First Steps to Success In Outside Sales

Copyright © 2002, 2018, Dave Kahle. All rights reserved.

No part of this publication may be reproduced, stored in a retrieval system or transmitted in any way by any means, electronic, mechanical, photocopy, recording or otherwise without the prior permission of the author except as provided by USA copyright law.

This publication is designed to provide accurate and authoritative information in regard to the subject matter covered. It is sold with the understanding that the publisher is not engaged in rendering legal, accounting or other professional service. If legal advice or other expert assistance is required, the services of a competent professional person should be sought.

Published by Dave Kahle Management, LLC P.O. Box 523; Comstock Park, MI 49321
1.616.451.9377

ISBN 9781976870774

CONTENTS

1. Introduction — 1
2. The Big Picture — 7
3. Your First Months — 21
4. Acquiring Appointments — 37
5. Making a Sales Call Part I — 57
6. Making Your First Sales Call Part II — 67
7. Your First Sales Call Part II — 85
8. Your First Sales Call Part III — 97
9. Developing Account Strategies — 107
10. Expanding the Business With Customers — 121
11. Managing Your Territory — 135
12. Managing Yourself — 149

ONE

1. Introduction

Objective

Based on the assumption that you are new to outside sales, this book is designed to provide you a deep under-standing of the principles, the processes, the techniques, and the tools that you will need in order to become successful as an outside (field) salesperson.

The professional salesperson—a personal insight

Before we get into the heart of the material, I'd like to share some of my thoughts and feelings about the job of the salesperson. I consider myself a professional salesperson – 30+ years of experience.

I had my first sales experience when I was seventeen years old. I got a job selling men's clothing in an expensive men's clothing store, working full time while I and going to college full time. Much of what I know today began in that environment of selling suits and sport coats on commission.

From there I went to selling for Jewel Tea Company, the forerunner of the Jewel grocery stores in the Chicago area. The company originated in the 1800s selling coffee and tea to housewives from horse-drawn carts. Later, it evolved into a national organization of hundreds of panel trucks selling a variety of groceries and household items to housewives on a route. I worked for them during the summers, selling groceries and house wares out of a Jewel Tea truck.

My first full-time professional sales experience came later when I sold amplification equipment to classrooms of hearing impaired children. It was a wonderful experience and a good company. I learned a great deal, as I did in all of my sales positions. In that position, I was fortunate enough to become the number one salesperson in the country for that company.

From there I moved to a really unusual selling situation. I sold surgical staplers. The staplers were used in surgical cases to staple organs back together during major surgery. At the time that I sold them, the concept was new, and surgeons did not know how to use them. Part of our job as salespeople, therefore, was to train them in how to use these new instruments. It was a fun and challenging job. Here's how we would sell them.

First, we would gain permission to be in the hospital. With this established, we then had to gain permission from the operating supervisor to be in the operating room. That was always difficult because the operating room supervisor was the strongest, toughest lady in the hospital. After she gave us permission to be in her domain, we'd work our way into the surgeons' locker room, where the surgeons changed out of their street clothes and into surgical greens. We'd do the same thing – get out of our street clothes, and put on surgical greens so we'd look like a doctor. We'd hang around the surgeons'

1. Introduction

locker room waiting for the right doctor to come in. When the right one came in and was in the middle of pulling on his pants and couldn't get away, we'd approach him, and show him the staplers. We were trained to say, "Doctor, if you'd like to try this, I'd be happy to scrub your next case with you."

"Scrubbing your next case" meant that we were one of those people, like you have seen on TV or the movies, who wash their hands and arms in a special way, walk in back-wards to the operating room suite with hands in the air, and have the nurses gown and gloves them. We were part of the operating room sterile team.

When it came time for the staplers to be used in the surgical procedure, we would be there, right across from the surgeon, to explain how to use those instruments. It was not until that point that a sale was actually made. That was a unusual and exciting sales experience.

From there, I recruited salespeople for a while. In that capacity, I interviewed thousands of salespeople and hundreds of sales managers.

Next, I went to work for a wholesale distributor. I worked for that company for a number of years and became the number one salesperson in the nation for the second time in my career. In 1988, I formed my own business and have been selling consulting and training services for my company ever since.

In all this 30-plus years of sales experience, I have al-ways maintained my enthusiasm for the job and for the challenge of being a professional salesperson. I have appreciated the many benefits that come with being a professional salesperson.

The job of the salesperson offers a lifetime of challenge. There are very few jobs that offer a continuous, never ending challenge. In the world of sales you are never as good as you can be, so you have a lifetime of challenge to continually improve yourself.

Let's not forget freedom. There are very few positions in this world where someone is as free to arrange their day and to make decisions about their work as the professional salesperson is. Of course, with that freedom comes responsibility. In many cases, an outside salesperson is responsible for millions of dollars of revenue for their employer. And that revenue supports and provides jobs and opportunities for several other families of employees in that company.

Additionally, professional salespeople have the opportunity for documentable, measurable achievement. In most positions in this world, it's very difficult to identify the achievement of any particular individual. But with field sales, the achievement can be measured in black and white, indisputable numbers. That achievement gives the salesperson a feeling of satisfaction and fulfillment that is one of the major fringe benefits to the career.

Then of course, there are friends. As an outside sales-person, you have daily opportunities to interact with all sorts of people. If you do a good job at it, many of those people will develop a relationship with you and turn into friends.

1. Introduction

Finally, there's the benefit that generally stimulates most people to enter the field -- money. If you compare sales to all the other kinds of jobs available, you'll find that outside sales almost always offers an opportunity for greater income than almost anything else that you can do.

To review, the benefits of becoming a professional salesperson include:

- unlimited challenge

- great freedom

- opportunity for documented achievement

- great responsibility

- the opportunity to build friends

- opportunity to make an income larger than most people.

That's quite a list.

TWO

2. The Big Picture

Objective

In this chapter we're going to examine the big picture that surrounds your job as an outside salesperson. This will give you a perspective from which to view the specific instructions we'll be discussing throughout the balance of this course.

The job of the field salesperson

Let's begin by defining your job. Why did your company hire you? What is your job all about? Why does your company have someone in your position after all?

If you boil the job of the professional salesperson down to its essence, it is this – to bring money into the business. Everything else is a means to that end. Yes, you take care of customers. Yes, you find new ones. Yes, you fix your customers' problems. Yes, you do all those, and other, things. However, all of those are a means to an end and peripheral to the core of the job. The end is this: to bring revenue into the company. If you don't bring money into the company, your job as a professional salesperson is at risk.

Understanding, then, that the ultimate purpose of your job is to bring money into the company, the question then becomes, "How do you do that?"

The answer to that question is, of course, what the rest of this course is all about.

Let's begin by understanding the primary sales process. There are certain basic processes, which give shape to your job. You create revenue for your company by managing dozens or hundreds of people through these core processes. As you successful do that, the net result is revenue.

The core sales processes

Look at illustration number one, The Basic Sales Process. Notice that there are five different steps to the sales process.

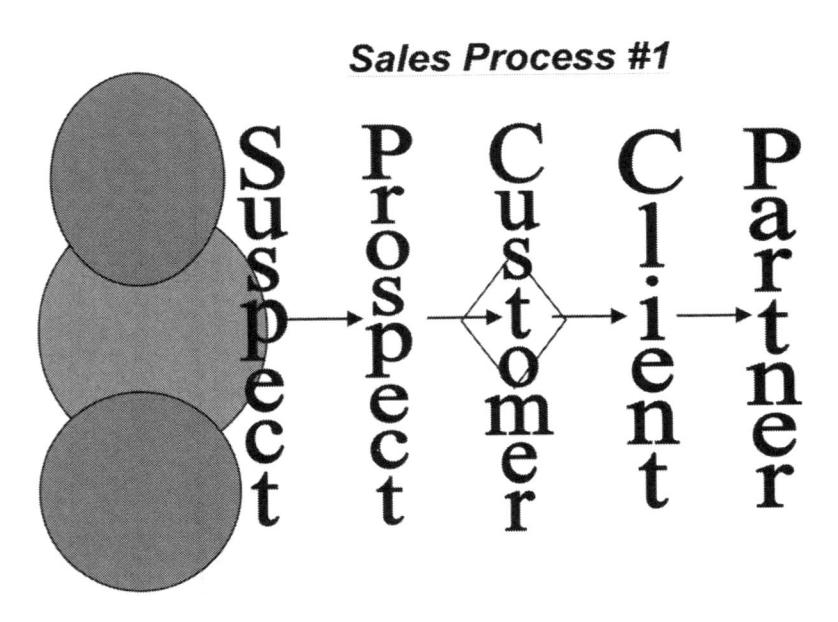

Sales Process #1

Suspect → Prospect → Customer → Client → Partner

On the far left-hand side of this diagram is that darkened area that I call "the land of complete apathy and total ignorance." That's

2. The Big Picture

where the people live who you suspect might one day do business with you. They go about their workdays blissfully ignorant of you. They don't know that you exist, so they're ignorant of you. They don't care that you exist, so they are apathetic.

The first part of your job is to identify some of the people in the land of apathy and ignorance who you suspect might one day do business with you. We call these people suspects. A suspect is someone you suspect may one day do business with you. There is something about that person that attracts your attention. Usually, it is that they work in a certain type or size of organization. As a salesperson, you scour the landscape of your territory and identify some of those suspects. You pluck out of "the land of apathy and ignorance" some companies or accounts that you think might one day do business with you. That's step one.

You move suspects through a screening process of some kind, and thus identify some of them as prospects. What's a prospect? A prospect is, first, an individual who works for an organization that has a legitimate need or interest in what you're selling. Secondly, an individual who is able to make or influence the decision to purchase your product. Thirdly, someone who has the ability to pay for your product or service. Step two of the sales process is to examine suspects and identify some of those who are prospects.

The next step in the salesperson's job description is to turn a prospect into a customer. A customer is someone who gives you money for what you have. When money changes hands, the relationship changes dramatically. That account has taken a risk in order to do business with you. You and your company are now known entities. Before they bought from you for the first time, you were an unknown. When they gave you money, the relationship shifted dramatically; you've now created a customer. Good for you, but you're not finished with them yet.

Now your job is to turn a customer into a client. A client is a customer who continually buys, over and over again. When you have developed the relationship to this point, you might think you're finished with them, that you have taken them as far as you can. Not true. There's one more step.

You're going to turn a client into a partner. What's a partner?

First, note that we are not using the word partner in the sense of a legal partnership agreement, although there could be a written document that solidifies the relationship. A partner is a company or individual who buys everything they can from you. A partner trusts you to a greater degree than any of your competitors. A partner exchanges more information with you and brings you into the sales process when a need is still just a concept in their minds. A partner is very, very close to you, prefers doing business with you, gives you referrals to other people, and in fact, is one of your single most productive relationships. That's a partner.

So, the "big picture" of your job as a salesperson is this: You move people through a series of steps in a relationship, bringing more and more of your suspects, slowly, over a period of time, into a partner

2. The Big Picture

relationship with you. As a result, they buy your company's products and you generate revenue for your employer. You identify people whom you suspect might one day do business with you; you then eliminate some of those and promote others into prospects; you turn prospects into customers, customers into clients, and clients into partners.

Level II Sales Processes

Understanding that your job is to transform suspects into partners, the next question is, "How do you do that?" Let's take it down to one more level of detail by breaking this big picture of "turning suspects into partners" into two pieces.

There are two essential, primary sales processes that are subsets of the fundamental process. Let's call them Level II sales processes. The first involves creating a customer, and the second involves expanding the business with a current customer.

Let's begin by focusing on key sales process number two – creating a customer. How do you create a customer? Look at illustration number two.

Typical Sales Process: Business-to-Business

Sales Process #2 – Creating a Customer

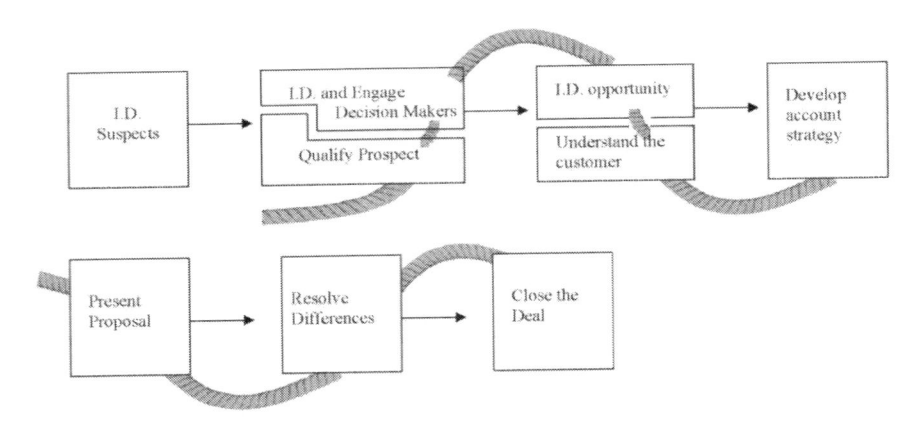

```
[I.D. Suspects] → [I.D. and Engage Decision Makers / Qualify Prospect] → [I.D. opportunity / Understand the customer] → [Develop account strategy]

[Present Proposal] → [Resolve Differences] → [Close the Deal]
```

Step one is to identify some suspects. Remember, a suspect is an account or an individual that you suspect might one day turn into a customer.

Once you have identified a suspect, you then must determine if they are qualified. In other words, you must determine if that company or individual is a prospect. You need to determine if this account can really purchase from you, if there is a legitimate need or interest in what you sell, and if the person you are speaking with can make or influence the decision.

Sometimes you can make that determination from the outside, without ever having met someone from that company. At other times, you may need to identify and engage the decision-makers. When I say engage, I mean that you meet face-to-face and interact with those people who make decisions about your product, service or program.

Which happens first, the qualification or the first interaction,

2. The Big Picture

depends on the situation. But both must happen before you can move onto the next step of the process.

Once you have qualified that prospect and engaged the decision-makers, then you move to the next step in the process -- understanding the customer as deeply and as thoroughly as you possibly can. In the process of understanding the customer, you're hopefully going to identify an opportunity for your product or service.

After you have gained an understanding of the customer, you next develop an account strategy. That means that you think about how you're going to sell this account now that you know them. You consider the question, "How are you going to influence them to buy your product or service?" The answer to that question becomes your strategy for your next step.

At some point in time, that strategy is going to mean that you're going to present an offer to them. An offer is an opportunity to purchase from you. The better job you do in each of the earlier steps -- qualifying, engaging the decision-makers, understanding, and identifying an opportunity -- the easier it is to present your offer and to make a proposal to this company. And the more likely it is that they will buy.

Once you've made the proposal, there are often some differences between what your customer wants and what you have offered. These often take the form of price, delivery, terms, and etc. They often are generated by the prospect comparing your offer to a competitor's offer.

These differences need to be resolved, and that forms the next step. When you successfully resolve all the differences and doubts in your customers mind, you naturally close the sale. And when you close that first sale you have converted a suspect into a customer. You will have completed the first of the two level II sales processes.

There's yet one more major sales process. The third sales process is called "expanding the business with a customer." Once a prospect has purchased something from you, that person is no longer a prospect. He has become a customer. Your job is not over, it has only just begun. Now you must influence that customer to purchase on a regular basis. As you create those additional sales, you move the customer closer and closer into a relationship with you.

Illustration number three graphically illustrates the steps in this process.

Typical Sales Process: Business to Business
Sales Process #3 - Expanding the Business with a Customer

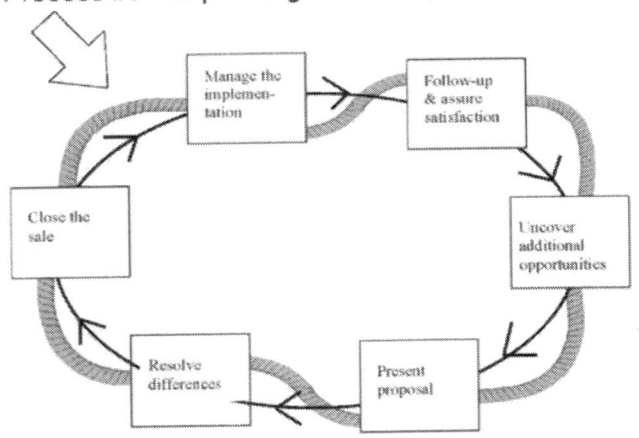

- Manage the implementation
- Follow-up & assure satisfaction
- Uncover additional opportunities
- Present proposal
- Resolve differences
- Close the sale

This process begins where the previous one ended -- with the

2. The Big Picture

order. You begin this process by managing the implementation. In other words, you make sure that that initial order goes well. You manage whatever it is you need to do. If you need to talk to your customer service department, or get a credit application filled out, or request extra inventory -- whatever it is that you need to do, doing it comprises the next step. Your focus is to ensure that the implementation of the first order goes well.

Once your customer has received whatever it is they've purchased from you, you proceed to the next step by following up on that initial purchase with the customer, and making sure that your customer is satisfied. Your objective is to hear the customer say, "Yes, we're satisfied," "Yes, it went well," "Yes, your stuff does what it's supposed to do."

Having assured that the customer is satisfied, you leverage that affirmation in order to identify additional opportunities. The assumption is that they can buy either more of what they originally purchased or they can buy additional categories of things from you. Your job at this point is to identify the specifics of those additional opportunities. Because of the growth in the relationship that has occurred throughout these two processes, it's easier now to identify additional opportunities than it was to identify that first one.

As you identify additional opportunities you bring in additional proposals. You resolve the differences, and you close the sale. That loop continues as long as the customer has needs. As you do that well, your customer becomes a client, your client becomes a partner, and you become more successful as a salesperson.

Those are the three primary sales processes. As a professional sales person, you will spend your career managing those processes over and over again with a wide variety of people.

The thread that ties it all together

Notice that there is a thread that runs through these sales processes. That thread is the quality of the relationship that develops between you and the customer. One of the reasons that people buy, particularly in business-to-business settings where they are buying over and over again, is because of their relationship with the company and the people who sell for that company.

Creating ever-growing relationships is not an event. It cannot be illustrated on the diagram as a step in the process. Rather, it's an ongoing process that is woven throughout the sales process from the beginning to the end. You begin to build that relationship when you say, "Hello" the first time. Every time you communicate with that customer, whether it's in writing, over the phone, or in person, you are building or detracting from that relationship.

One of the most important competencies for a professional salesperson is the skill of continually building powerful, strong relationships. Why is that important? People do business with people they trust. Don't you? If you are shopping for something, and there's something about the salesperson that gives you a bad feeling, are you going to be comfortable spending money with that person? If you are

2. The Big Picture

like most of us, you're going to look for someone else. People do business with people they trust, and people do not do business with people they don't like and don't trust.

Here's an example of this from my own personal life. A number of years ago, my next-door neighbor had arranged for a lawn service to regularly fertilize his lawn. After a couple of seasons, his lawn looked noticeably better than mine. I became a little embarrassed by the difference between his lawn and mine. So I determined, one spring, that I would call that same company and have them come out and fertilize my lawn, too. I got the name of the company from him and called them. I was ready to buy – a qualified prospect.

I entered into a conversation with the salesperson on the phone, indicating that what I wanted to do was have them come out and do a first application of whatever it is they did, and then leave me some information about what my options were. I like to read about things instead of just hear about them. I wanted to see their program in writing. Then I'd make a decision as to what kind of program I wanted to commit to. I called and explained to them what I wanted to do, and gave them my address. The salesperson said, "Fine, we can do that, we'll give you a first application and then we'll leave some literature for you, and you can make a decision," and I said, "Great, that's what I would like to do." It was a deal.

Then he said, "Ok, let me just confirm that we'll be out by the end of next week, we'll do that application and then you can cancel anytime you want." I said, "What?" He said, "Well, yes, you can cancel anytime you want." I said, "Well, wait a minute, no. You don't understand, I'm not committing right now, I wanted to look at the programs you have and then make a decision."

Then he said, "Well, yes, but you can cancel at anytime you want after the first one." I said, "Wait a minute, I'm not committing to anything now other than the first application." He said, "Yes, but," and I said, "No," and he said, "Yes, but," and I said, "No," and I hung up.

Maybe I reacted a little too much, but the point is this: There was something about that conversation that made me not trust the person. First, he said it was OK to do it the way I wanted, and then he threw other things in that caused me to hesitate. I thought, "Hey, wait a minute, if I can't trust you on this small issue, I can't trust you on anything else, and since I can't trust you, I don't want to do business with you."

That's human nature. That's why the relationship between you and your customer – a relationship characterized by continuously growing trust -- is such an important part of the sales process. It begins when you say "Hello," and it never ends. The relationship is the thread that ties the process together.

Terms

suspect – an individual or organization that you suspect may one day do business with you.

prospect – an individual or organization that has a legitimate need or interest in what you're selling, has the ability to make or

2. The Big Picture

influence the decision to purchase your product and has the ability to pay for it.

customer – an individual or organization who has given you money for something you sell.

client – a customer who continually buys over and over again.

partner – a client who buys everything they can from you. A partner is someone who trusts you to a greater degree than any of your competitors, who exchanges more information with you; who brings you into the sales process when a need is still just a concept in their minds. A partner is a client who is very, very close to you, prefers doing business with you, gives you referrals to other people, and in fact, is one of your single most productive relationships.

qualify – the process of determining if a suspect is a prospect. Sometimes the terms prospect and qualified prospect will be used instead of suspect and prospect.

engage – to interact face-to-face with those people who make decisions about your product or service.

account strategy – the unique step-by-step plan for selling to a specific account.

offer – an opportunity to purchase something from you which you submit to a prospect or customer.

decision maker – an individual within an account who is totally or partially responsible for making the decision as to whether or not to purchase your product or service.

sales process – a step-by-step series of actions on the part of the prospect/customer for which the salesperson is responsible. Generally results in some measurable outcome.

ggestions in this chapter as a compliment to what your supervisor may suggest for you.

Where to start?

Begin by focusing on four different tasks in the first few months of your activity.

First, conscientiously build relationships with people within your organization who will later be very instrumental to your success.

Second, gain some hands-on familiarity with applications of the products you sell. It's one thing to learn about the products through manuals, samples and demonstrations, and it's another to understand your products' applications — how your customers use the products or services you sell.

Third, engage in activities that will build your own personal confidence and competence.

Finally, identify those customers and prospects with whom you can immediately work. In the first few months of your job, you're going to find some people that are very open to you and others that are not. You should use the first few months to identify those people with whom you can gain the quickest response.

Those are the four primary tasks to focus on as you begin to organize yourself for the first few months of your job. You may now be thinking, "Hey. Wait a minute. There isn't any mention of selling anything." That's right. I haven't said anything about selling because I don't believe that is your highest priority in the first few months of your job. Certainly it's great if you can bring in some orders, but I'm more interested in you laying the groundwork for exceptional success in the future. If you do the things that I'm going to suggest you do here, you will gain sales as a result.

FOUR TASKS EXAMINED

1. Build relationships with your people.

Your first task is to build relationships with people within your organization who can be helpful to you later on. One of the roles that you will play in your job as a field salesperson is that of an advocate for your customers. You will bring your customers' concerns and problems back to your organization and try to solve problems and provide services for those customers.   So, you're going to need to know people inside your organization who can help you. That's an important part of your job. Use this time now, when you have a little extra time, to build strong relationships with those instrumental, important people inside your organization. It's going to be much more difficult to do it six months from now when you're overwhelmed with things to do and just don't have time to sit down and chat with a customer service representative or someone in purchasing, marketing, or the warehouse. Those are the kinds of people with whom you need to build relationships now.

Attack this project by systematically thinking about who in your organization can help you in the future. Ask the other salespeople to identify the key people. Talk to your supervisor and gain his/her input. Create a list of the people you need to know well, and then make it a point to spend some time with each one.

Find out what do they do, and what kind of problems they have with other salespeople. Ask how you can help them when it's time for them to be involved with you. How can you present your problems in a way that they can appreciate? Come to know them, showing some concern and interest in them. The relationship that you build now with all these people inside your company will be tremendously beneficial to you later.

I had to learn this one the hard way. At the point where I began one of my sales positions, I had been a very successful salesperson. I had the habit of coming into the office regularly, and dropping work on peoples' desks, just assuming, of course, that they'd do that because, after all, that was their job.

I didn't know this at the time, but I was generating resentment among the people I was working with. It got to the point that the operations manager went to my boss, the branch manager, and said, "We've got to do something about Kahle. He's a problem. People resent him." The branch manager came to me and said, "David, you must change your ways. You are aggravating some of the people."

I listened to him, and thought to myself, "Well, I'm a heavy hitter around here, and as long as my sales are good, it's OK." I went on my way and did not change my ways. A month or so later the operations manager began lobbying my boss to get me fired because I was creating havoc when I came into the office and assumed everybody was going to jump to help me. The branch manager once again sat me down and said, "Listen. This is serious. You need to mend your ways. You need to treat the people inside the organization with more courtesy."

This time I took him to heart. I thought, "OK. I better do something because my job is being threatened."

Here's what I did. At that time Stroh's Signature beer had just been introduced and was incredibly popular and very hard to buy. It was rationed to the retail stores. However, I found a way to purchase a six-pack of Stroh's Signature beer for each of the people inside the organization whom I had offended with my brash manner.

I gave each of them a six-pack, apologized, and tried to get the relationship back to a better place. It worked, but it was enormously difficult for me to do. If I would have taken what I now see as good advice -- to build relationships with those people when you have the opportunity -- it would have been a much smoother, easier situation for me.

2. One strategy to accomplish the next three tasks.

Your second task is to understand, first hand, the applications of your products and services. It's one thing to read brochures and technical specifications, but it's quite a different thing to see the product in use and hear about your services or your products from your customers' perspective.

In addition, you need to do some things to gain some confidence and competence, and, at the same time, to identify some

...ple that you can begin to work with. You can do all of these by following one strategy.

Visit some of your customers and see how they actually use your products and services. Talk to the people who are using them. Your goal is to gain first hand knowledge so that in a month or two from now you can say to someone else, "Well, so and so uses it this way. So and so has this application," and you will be speaking with competence and confidence. That will make you much more credible. Use the time now to gain some of that knowledge and credibility by seeing your product in use.

Begin by calling on your current customers first, and start with the smaller of those. After you have visited your smaller customers, you can work your way up to the larger ones. Introduce yourself and explain that you're new. Ask them to help you to learn how to take better care of them. Ask for their help. Specifically, ask these eight questions of those customers:

1. "Tell me about your business." This is the first step in learning about their business. Listen carefully to their response. Remark about anything that is unique or unusual. Ask some more specific questions as they occur to you. Then ask about the person with whom you are talking by using the second question.

2. "And what do you do?" After listening respectfully, move on to

3. Your First Months

the third question.

3. "What's been your experience with my company?" That's an open-ended question that should prompt them to explain quite a bit. Again, your job is to just listen, to learn from your customers. Don't be defensive, be inquisitive.

4. "Which of our products are you using?"

5. "And how is that going?"

6. "Could I see…" and then you fill in the blank. In other words, if they're using one of your products in the production department, you say, "Could I see it?" Or if they are making use of some service, you could say, "Could I talk with the person who's involved with that?" Your objective is to go into that area of the business where people are actually using your product or service, and see it hands-on being used. Then you'll be able to say to some other customer, "You know at so and so they're doing it this way."

7. "Is there anything we can do to improve our services for you?" Listen carefully and take good notes.

8. "What issues are you working on that we might be involved in?" You are basically asking them to tell you how you can sell to them.

Those are eight specific questions, word for word, that can form your first set of sales calls to good customers.

After you have asked these eight questions and learned a great deal from your customer, end the interaction by asking the customer to agree to see you again. Maybe you will even make an appointment for a specific time. Regardless, attempt to end the interaction with some kind of an agreement.

After you leave the customer's place of business, sit down in your car and take notes. Capture the knowledge that you've just gained. You'll need to organize this information by adhering to some very specific disciplines. You'll need to develop a contact log, a 'to do" list, and an account profile.

Contact Log

The contact log can be something as simple as a yellow pad, or as complex as an entry into an Internet-based contact manager system. Regardless of the mechanics, you'll need to record the date, what you discussed with the customer, who you met and talked to, and what you intend to discuss the next time you're there. If you're computerized, your contact management software will organize your notes. If you are not, then you need to create a file system to keep these notes organized. For now, create a manila folder for each customer, and tear off the yellow pad notes and place them inside that customer's folder.

To Do List

As you think about the sales call and the conversations you had, it may be that there are some things that you need to do as a result. You may have promised the customer to look into some lingering problem, or find the specifications for a new product, or research a special price, etc. Now is the time to capture those notes in a separate document. Again, if you are computerized, you can use your system's "to do" function. If not, then start a separate document on which you consolidate all of the day's tasks. That way, you'll have all your notes about things you must do in a single location.

At this point you will have created an account contact log that captures the conversation and what you're going to do next. You also have a "to do" list of the things you need to accomplish before you see this customer again.

Account Profile

Finally, fill in any blanks on your account profile form that you able. It could be that you already have an account profile, that your company uses one, and that you've inherited those account profiles for all of your customers. If so, good for you

If not, then you need to create this powerful tool.

What's an account profile form? It's a document. If you are

computerized, it's several screens on your contact manager. If you are not computerized, then it's a piece of paper. On this piece of paper are blanks for you to fill in. These blanks are used to capture useful information about your customer. The reason you use this account profile is that it forces you to be thorough in your collection of information about the account.

You may have read the book Swimming With Sharks by Harvey McKay. In that book, the author talks about the "McKay 66". What's the "McKay 66"? It's his version of an account profile form. The "McKay 66" contains sixty-six questions, or more accurately, places to put sixty-six answers to questions. It's a form. Every salesperson must complete every item for every key person in every account. It's a requirement of the job. If you are going to be a salesperson for that company, you are going to complete the form.

You may now be thinking, "Sixty-six questions? Where could I possibly get sixty-six things?" By the time you're done completing a "McKay 66" you know where that customer has gone to school and what sports teams he follows, if any. You know what the person's hobbies are. You know what the political affiliation. You know their religious affiliation. You know how important that is to them. You know where their kids go to school. You know the name of their spouse as well as the names of the kids. You know this person in detail and in thoroughness.

Sixty-six questions may be a bit of an overkill. However, the principle is powerful and useful. If your company doesn't provide one,

3. Your First Months

you need to develop your own account profile form, and then discipline yourself to use it methodically.

What kind of information do you need to collect on your account profile form? Let's start with the basic information. Name - first and last name. Address, phone number of the key contact people within that account, then maybe the names and phone numbers and extensions of their assistants and associates. After you have recorded the basic information move on.

Think about what would be useful for you to know. It would be useful for you to know what categories of product or service each customer purchased. It would be useful to know what other competitors they deal with. It would be useful to know how they go about making a decision and who is on the decision making team, if there is such a thing. To create this form, you just ask yourself, "What would be useful to know about this account?" You then create a form, put a place for that information in the form, and then try to collect that information.

Why is this so important? For a number of reasons. It gives you an organized and thorough way to collect information. If you don't have some thorough, organized system, you're probably going to revert to a haphazard, on again, off again, information collecting approach. When you are on again, off again, that reflects in your performance. You ought to have a system and do things thoroughly. That's number one.

Secondly, the account profile provides a place to store

information other than in your head. You can probably remember a lot of things. But if you make a sales call at eight o'clock in the morning, by four o'clock in the afternoon, much of the detail of that call is gone. If you are not going to see this customer again for a month, much of what you talked about will have faded from your memory. You need to have that knowledge and information in a form that you can refer to instead of just relying on your memory.

Thirdly, using an account profile form appears very professional to your customer. When you explain to the customer that you need to ask some questions, and then you begin to ask some questions and fill in your account profile form, your customer gets the impression that you are very thorough and professional about what you do. Almost always the use of an account profile form is seen by the customer as a positive reflection on you.

Then there's one more reason. That is the use of a form like this drives the communication process to deeper levels. In other words, when you force yourself to ask certain questions, you create communication between you and your customer. Often, you would not have that communication if it weren't for the form. For example, maybe your form says something like this: "What is this company's three-year strategic plan? Fill it in here."

In order to do so, you must ask about their three-year strategic plan. This drives you to specific conversation with your customer. You ask, "Where do you want this business to go three years from now?" That's a good conversation to have. That's a deep, worthwhile,

3. Your First Months

significant conversation to have. If you had not have had the form, you may never have asked that question, and you probably never would have had that kind of communication. So, the use of the form drives deeper communication.

Here's how you can create your account profile form. Begin by thinking about the different kinds of customers you call on. Group them in to segments, or groups of customers that have something in common. Then, for each segment, ask yourself, "What kind of information would be nice to have? What would I like to know about this company or this customer?" Create a form for all of those pieces of information. Then try to collect that information, and complete the form.

You will discover that some of the information is easy for you to collect. Some other information may be too difficult to easily obtain. So after a little bit of use, you'll refine the form.

Begin immediately to gain the experience of using it, and expect that you will make changes as you go.

Create the form, duplicate it so that you have one for every customer, and begin to use it.

Create two versions. The account profile itself, which is the form that collects information about the customer, the company, or the organization to which you're selling. The second part is the personal profile. The personal profile focuses on information about the individuals within the account. So you might have a large account, where there are five key decision-makers. You will have one account profile for the company and five separate ones for each of the five key contacts. The personal profile is for personal information like where they went to school, their political affiliations, the organizations they belong to, what they like to talk about, where they went on their last vacation, etc.

One other question that people often ask is, "How do I actually collect this information?" For the account information, you can generally sit down with a clipboard in your hand and fill out the form, asking your customer specific questions. That will work for the account information. But you cannot do that with the personal information. To collect personal information, you look through your form before you make a sales call in order to be sensitive to the pieces of information that come up in the conversation. When you sit down in your car after the sales call to consolidate your notes, you then fill in those blanks. After the next sales call you fill in a few more blanks. It can take you several months to complete a personal profile. However, at that point the information is there for you to use and refer to as you go about your business from here on out.

So an account profile, in both of its versions -- the account version and the personal version -- is something that you ought to create right away and begin to use immediately.

After your first initial calls, you'll spend a few moments in the car taking notes and capturing the knowledge that you've gained as you methodically work through your customer base. By the time you are

3. Your First Months

finished going through your customer base and visiting each customer, you will have accomplished the other three objectives. You will have gained an understanding of product application; you will now have a great understanding of the details of how your product is used in real life. You will have gained confidence and competence.

Finally, you will have identified some people who have opportunities for you. These are the people who you can begin to work with.

You will have accomplished that in the first few months of your job. You will have laid the groundwork for a very successful career by focusing on some of the learning issues in these first few months.

As you start with the small customers and move up to the large, the information you gather and the experience you gain will help you develop confidence and competence. By the time you start walking into those larger customers, you will be able to talk about products are actually used, and you'll know how other people are using it. You'll be much more confident yourself.

Later, after you've gone through your customer list, you can start calling on prospects.

That's an issue we will deal with later.

Terms

account profile – a document, either electronic or paper, containing blanks for you to insert useful information about your prospect or customer.

product (service) applications – the specific uses of your product or service; the way your customers actually use what you sell.

good sales question – a well-phrased question, asked by a salesperson of a prospect or customer which serves to facilitate some part of the sales process.

personal profile – that portion of an account profile on which information about the individuals within that account is stored.

contact log – a document on which you record the things you discussed with the prospect/customer, and the things that you want to discuss the next time you are together.

"to do" list – a document on which you list the things you must do as a result of our sales calls.

FOUR

4. Acquiring Appointments

Objective

In this chapter we're going to consider one of the core competencies for outside sales success – a competency that you can use almost every day for the rest of your career. You'll use it when you're attempting to see suspects and prospects as well as when you want to talk to customers, clients and partners. The subject of this chapter is the competency of acquiring appointments.

The importance of acquiring appointments

It is more difficult today to see your prospects and customers than it was a few years ago, and it will continue to grow more difficult. There was a time when you could just stop by unannounced, and almost everyone would see you. But in today's time-starved world where your customers have more and more constraints on their time, they must manage their time more tightly. And that means that they don't have the luxury of seeing every salesperson who stops by. They must be jealous of their time, and invest it only by appointment with those salespeople who they believe bring some value to them.

So, let's begin our analysis of this competency by thinking about the task. Let's start by focusing on an objective. What is it that you want to accomplish? You may be thinking, "That's easy. My objective is to make an appointment."

Good start. It sounds so simple, but it is often the lack of this clear understanding that hinders salespeople. Many make the mistake of trying to sell their product over the phone. When you pick up that phone to call a prospect or customer, your objective is to make an appointment -- it is not to sell your product over the phone. Nor is it to sell your company over the phone. Your objective is to give the person a reason to see you. Everything else will come later.

Five Step Process

In order to gain competence at this crucial aspect of your job, you need to practice the discipline of working through a five-step process.

Step One: Determine who to call.

This sounds so simple; yet executing this step well is often overlooked. It is a waste of valuable time and effort to call the wrong people. So you need to be sure that you are calling the right people. And who might they be? Here's a very simple criterion: You should call people who can make the decision to buy your product, or, as a subset, people who can influence the decision.

This is not as simple and obvious as it may seem. Here's how to effectively create a list of the "right people" to talk to.

Begin by identifying those organizations who are suspects. Create an extensive list.

4. Acquiring Appointments

Then, do some research. Use the Internet, databases, Dunn & Bradstreet, talk to people in your organization who might know those companies, and find out something about each of those organizations before you call on them. Find out what they make or what they do, the names of some of their major customers, what their mission or vision statements are, and, if possible, the names of some of the people who make or influence the decision about the products and services that you sell.

Then make a list of the names of those individuals who you think may be important to see. Add their company names and the phone numbers. This list can be on paper or in an electronic file. Regardless, it is the beginning of a never-ending process. You should continually update the list with new names whenever you discover some. This prospect list is one of your assets, and continually updating it and adding to it is an essential discipline. While you are beginning to develop your list now, you will never finish the task. Continually looking for additional prospects and adding them to the list is a regular discipline you should follow for the rest of your career.

It may be that you can only rarely obtain the right person's name. When you cannot gain a specific name, follow these guidelines. The ideal situation is one in which you know the first and last name of the person you want to speak to. But that is not always possible. If you don't have a first and last name, the second best situation is calling someone by their job title. In other words, instead of saying "May I speak to Bill Smith," you say, "May I speak to the production manager." If you are unsure of the appropriate job title, then the third best situation is "the person who…" In this situation, when you call you say, "May I speak to the person who purchases…" whatever it is you are selling. So there are three levels of quality in your list. The first level is the person's name, second is the job title, and third is the "person who purchases…" whatever it is that you have to sell.

After you have created a list, prioritize it. Keep some guidelines in mind. First, remember that it's always more effective for you to go from the top down than from the bottom up. Try to make an appointment with the highest-level person in the organization that you are targeting. In other words, in smaller organizations, try the president first. You may get him on the phone. In that case, he/she may say, "Listen. I'm not going to have time for you. Talk to so and so." Then you can call so and so and say the president suggested you call him. In larger organizations, try to identify the person who is at the top of the ladder in the department or area that you are concerned with and try that person first.

If you have attempted to reach the top person and were not successful, the second priority is to attempt to reach the easiest person to talk to in that organization. There are, within almost every organization, people whose job it is to talk to salespeople. These can be purchasing agents, office managers, or similar job titles. After you have some experience in your job, you'll be able to identify these people.

Step Two: Deliver an optional "pre-call touch."

You may choose to use a pre-call touch prior to calling for the

4. Acquiring Appointments

appointment. A pre-call touch is some communication to the person that you want to talk to which is designed to make that person more receptive to your call.

There are several different kinds of pre-call touches. The first and most effective is a personal introduction. If you know someone who can introduce you personally, face-to-face, to the person you want to talk to, that personal introduction is always the most effective way of meeting a new person. Once you have your list, look through the names and ask yourself, "Is there anyone I know who might know some of these people?" If so, ask them to introduce you. If they agree, then you will have arranged for a very effective pre-call touch.

Next down the ladder of effectiveness is an introductory phone call. This is where someone you know calls someone who is on the list and suggests to them that they talk to you when you call. They introduce you over the phone and say good things about you. That's another very effective pre-call touch.

Here's a third one, called a pre-heat letter. This is a letter from someone else, to the person who you want to see, introducing you. In other words, instead of you just calling the person out of the cold, you have someone write them a letter. This isn't as hard as it seems. My insurance agent does this with me. Here's how he works his system...

He calls and invites me to lunch once or twice a year. Of course I know that he wants to get some referrals from me.

After I agree to have lunch with him, he sends me a form a few days before the lunch. The form asks very specific questions, all asking who I know who meets certain criteria. My job is to list some names on this form. Then we go to lunch. At lunch we make small talk and catch up on each other's lives. Then somewhere toward the end of the lunch, my insurance agent pulls out his big folder and he says, "Now who do you know who I might see?" He asks me to refer to the form and read off the list of names.

So, I give him two or three names. That, however, is not the end of it. He next asks me about each of those people. He inquires into what I know about them, how old they are, what education they have, do they own their own business, etc. He collects pieces of information about each of those people. Then he says, "You wouldn't mind introducing me to them, would you?"

I say, "No. I guess not."

He says, "How about if I write a letter from you to them mentioning me and suggesting that if I call them that they should take the call? I will write a letter from you and I'll have my secretary bring it over, all you have to do is sign it. Would that be OK?"

I agree to do that. Sometime in the next couple of days in comes the secretary with two or three letters from me to the people whose names I just gave him, introducing my insurance agent to them. I sign them and she folds them up, slides them into an envelope and off they go. That's a great example of a pre-call touch, a letter from someone else that introduces you and conditions that person to accept your call.

4. Acquiring Appointments

Here's another type of pre-call touch: A series of deliveries that come from you that softens the prospect and makes them more likely to receive your call. You can create a series of letters, or other creative deliveries, and send one, two, three, four, five letters beforehand, each emphasizing some aspect of what it is you sell. And by the time your prospect has read those letters or received your deliveries they should be open to talking to you.

I have a great example from a client of mine who created this kind of program. You'll find it to be very creative. Here's how it worked.

This company, an advertising agency, had their list of "right people". They had a hundred people, all qualified prospects with whom they wanted appointments. In the first week they sent each of them a small box wrapped in brown paper with no return address on it, and the prospect's address written in a woman's handwriting -- just a hand written address on the brown paper.

Each of the one hundred prospects received this box. When they opened the box, they found a lemon inside. Accompanying the lemon was a little slip of paper, like that which you get in fortune cookies. It read, "Don't let it go sour." That was it.

The next week, another box, looking exactly the same, was sent to the prospect. Inside it was a sugar cube and a little slip of paper that read, "Keep it sweet." Nothing else, just the sugar cube.

In week three, the box contained tinsel -- like that which you put on a Christmas tree. The note inside read, "Make it sparkle." That's all.

In week four, the box contained a business card from the salesperson with a note that read, "I'd like to make an appointment with you to discuss creative ways we can increase your business."

That was a very effective pre-call touch – a delivery to the prospect conditioning him/her to accept your call. In this case, the pre-call touch was one hundred percent effective. Everyone who received that mailing agreed to an appointment.

Here's another possibility, a fax or an email to your prospect first, giving the prospect some reason to take your call. Send a fax or email and then follow it up with a call.

Finally, another very effective pre-call touch is a handwritten, not a typed, not a computer generated letter, but a handwritten, personal letter from you to the prospect explaining what you would like to see them about and asking for an appointment.

Step Three: Prepare effective scripts.

Before you actually make the phone call, prepare, word-for-word, what you're going to say when someone answers that phone.

Your language will be far more effective and your results greatly improved if you prepare what you want to say before you make the call, instead of thinking that on the spur of the moment you can develop the most effective language.

Having an effective script prepared word for word frees you to

4. Acquiring Appointments

be more effective. If you don't know what you are going to say, you must make it up on the spur of the moment. The problem with that is that when the other person is talking, instead of listening carefully, you are thinking about what you are going to say. You are not focusing on what the person is saying; instead, you are focusing on what you are going to say next. That means that you are not doing a good job of listening. Because you don't listen well, you are not as sensitive to the customer as you ought to be.

On the other hand, when you have a script, you know exactly what you're going to say and you are, therefore, free to concentrate on the customer.

Begin by considering what is likely to happen when you make that phone call. One of three things will occur. First, you may get a gatekeeper. That is someone whose job it is to open the door or close the gate to people like you. Their boss doesn't necessarily want to talk to everybody who calls, so they have a gatekeeper, screen people and decide who the boss should talk to. The gatekeeper is often a receptionist or an assistant. It is much more likely though these days that you'll encounter voice mail. Occasionally, you might even get through to the right person in person.

You need to prepare a script for each of those three situations. That way, you'll be prepared for whatever situation you encounter.

STRATEGIES FOR EACH

Gatekeepers

There are proven strategies for each of these situations. Let's begin with the gatekeeper?

First, let's consider what not to do. Don't try to bully them, and don't be deceitful. I receive solicitation calls from stockbrokers almost every week. I don't want to talk to them. Occasionally, one manages to get past my gatekeepers by making them believe that it is a personal call, or that I know the stockbroker who is calling. I've often wondered if they have considered the likelihood of me trusting someone with my money whose very first interaction with me was based on deceit. Not very likely.

Don't use those kinds of tactics. Instead, make the gatekeeper into a friend. Learn the person's name, explain what it is you want to talk to the boss about, and ask the gatekeeper for help. "Can you help me?" is a very powerful appeal. Your gatekeeper script, then, should reflect this strategy of making them a friend.

Voice Mail

What happens when you get voice mail? First, always leave a message. Each time you leave a message your prospect is going to hear your name and the name of your company. If you leave four or five messages, he/she will hear your name and your company's name four or five times. Each time is like an advertising impression in that it makes an impression on your prospect's mind, just like all those

4. Acquiring Appointments

commercials for Coke or Ford.

Second, consider organizing your script like a memo. In a few short words, mention who you are, what your company does, what you want to discuss with him/her, and the benefit of returning your call.

Consider, also, organizing your script like a thirty-second radio commercial. If you had the ability to buy a radio commercial that would pinpoint that message and beam it directly to your prospect, what would you say? Voice mail gives you the opportunity to do just that. You have the opportunity to beam a thirty-second radio commercial directly to this person. In this commercial, you may give them the single most powerful benefit of calling you, or the single most painful problem that you think they have and the way in which you can solve it.

An additional strategy for dealing with voice mail is to simply make the appointment. In this case, your voice mail message says something like this: "I'm going to be in your area Tuesday at ten o'clock. I will see you then unless I hear otherwise."

The right person

On those rare occasions when you actually connect with the right person, your script should focus on five different items in a very short period of time. Introduce yourself, explain the purpose of your meeting with that person and what's in it for him/her. Then mention how much time you expect to take and then, ask for the appointment.

Step Four: Prepare for objections.

After you prepare your scripts for the appointment, you are not th your preparation. You now need to think through the someone is likely to give to you. For example, think to yourself, "Ok. If I say can I see you at two o'clock next week, what is he likely to say?"

What are the most common reasons that someone would say no? Maybe they would say they're too busy. That's one objection. Maybe they would say that they don't know anything about your company. That's another. You just place yourself in the mind of your prospect, and think through the reasons he or she may not want to see you.

When you have identified each of the top three or four reasons, the ones that you think you're going to hear most commonly, you then prepare a response for each of those objections. So, if he or she says, "Well, I'm awfully busy," you say, "I can appreciate that. You know we're all busy these days and it's because I value your time and I know you're busy that I only want to take ten minutes, no more than that, to see if we can't be of some help to you and save you time down the road. So, is Tuesday OK, or should I stop in and see you Wednesday?" What you've done is thought through how you're going to respond to objections before they actually arise.

Step Five: Implement effectively

You'll note that, to this point, each of the four previous steps has to do with preparation. If you have faithfully followed the four steps, you'll be fully prepared to effectively make appointments. The final step in the process is to implement this phone call effectively. Here

4. Acquiring Appointments

are some tips for effective implementation.

Number one, call early in the day. Most people are just generally a little more receptive early in the day. They haven't got the burden of the bulk of the day's activities on their mind. And if you call early in the day, then you can be available for people to call you back. If you call last thing in the afternoon, they're probably not going to call you back that day.

Two: If you're having difficulty getting through to someone, try calling before and after working hours. This is particularly effective if you are calling owners or bosses of smaller businesses, as they are almost always there before anyone else. If the business starts at eight o'clock, try calling at seven forty-five, and you're likely to get the boss.

Three: Have someone available who can answer your call if and when someone returns it. If you are going to make an hour's worth of calls, and then you are going to go out for the day, make sure that there's someone in the office who can answer the return calls and schedule those appointments for you. This prevents you playing phone tag for weeks with a prospect who is willing to see you.

Four. You may want to make a warm call first. A warm call is a call to someone you know, someone who likes you and be counted on to be receptive to your call. Call your boyfriend, girlfriend, spouse, child, etc. Talk for a few minutes. That will warm you up and help you be comfortable in anticipation of the next cold call. Immediately after you hang up on the warm call, dial that next number – your first cold call.

Five: Try standing when you make that phone call. There's something about standing that makes you a little more focused on what you're doing and helps you to concentrate. So rather than sit at a desk, try standing.

Six: Smile. Force yourself to smile. When you smile, that smile helps engender an attitude or a feeling within you. And that feeling is communicated in your voice. The person at the other end of the line can sense your attitude.

Seven: Make sure that you have all your calls ready, and make one immediately after the other. As you hang up from one, immediately start dialing the next one. Don't stop and think about it. Don't ruminate. Just hit those next numbers. This is one time when thinking about it will probably not be positive. So prevent yourself from thinking about the previous call by immediately making the next one.

What next?

What happens if you still can't make an appointment? Consider Plan B, the option of last resort. Plan B is physically stopping by, walking into the customer's location and see if you can, by your personal presence, make an appointment. Remember, you are not going to walk in and attempt to see someone; you are going to walk in and attempt to make an appointment to see someone. If the prospect appears to have significant enough potential to warrant that kind of investment of your time, than a personal visit is an option of last resort. It may work on occasions when nothing else will.

4. Acquiring Appointments

This happened to me a couple of weeks ago, while I was working in my office in downtown Grand Rapids. I'm in an inner office, with my staff in the outer office, which opens up the common hallway. A young man who wasn't over ten or twelve years old opened the door to the outer office, walked right passed my staff, opened the closed door to my inner office, walked in and announced that he was selling cookies for his fund raiser. There he was, right in front of me, giving me this pitch to buy his cookies. My response was, "How much?"

He said, "Four fifty a box." I said, "Ok. I'll take a box," and I did. He made the sale and walked right out. Everybody was speechless. That kind of thing just doesn't happen. But it worked. If he would have called he would have not had a chance in the world of getting in to see me, but he just walked right in. You may not be quite that brazen. But there is a time to risk that kind of investment of time and energy when you think it's worthwhile and there's nothing else that's working for you. Then you fall back on Plan B.

Managing Yourself

Let's consider for a moment what stands in your way when you attempt to acquire an appointment. We can put all possible hindrances into two basic categories: Your customer's situation and those things that reside in your mind.

Your customer may be busy with someone else when you call. He may have a lot of things on his mind. He may be talking with another person. He may be in the middle of some kind of project. He may be getting ready to leave to go to a meeting. All of those things, which you really are not aware of, hinder your ability to make that appointment. All of these are perfectly legitimate reasons why your prospect isn't going to talk to you or isn't going to say yes right this minute. And they all have to do with his situation -- not you.

In addition to the details of your customer's situation, there's another class of hindrances to your ability to make appointments, and those are those things that reside in yourself. The chief of these is fear.

You cannot do anything about the first set of circumstances. There's really very little you can do about what's happening with your customer. But, you can focus on the second – you.

You may find that, in spite of the preparation that you have done, you are still hesitant to pick up that phone and call. Why? Most likely, it is fear of failure and/or fear of rejection. Every salesperson, at some time or another, experiences that fear.

The fear of failure and the fear of rejection are the most common internal issues salespeople face. Having that fear is not unusual. Learning to handle that fear is one of the most useful skills of effective sales people.

Handling fear

Here are some suggestions about how to handle that fear.

First, recognize the issue. Acknowledge that what's happening is that you are afraid. You'd just rather not do this thing because you are afraid. Ok. The first step toward overcoming something is to acknowledge it. You are afraid. Recognize it and move on.

4. Acquiring Appointments

Now that you have acknowledged the source of your hesitancy, you must do something about it. Keep this phrase in mind. The phrase is, "Stop the thought." Let's analyze what is going on in your mind. You are thinking things to yourself, you're repeating some thoughts in your mind about how this isn't going to work, or you are thinking that you cannot get through to someone no matter what, or you're thinking that if you do get them on the phone, that person will be irritated and short with you. You are dwelling on negative thoughts.

When you realize you're doing that, you need to stop those thoughts. It's not the reality of the situation that is stopping you, it is your thoughts about it. The solution is, then, to stop thinking those negative things. One way to do that is to say to yourself, "Stop that thought." Don't let those thoughts go through your mind. Then, force more positive thoughts into your mind.

Here's another strategy. Remind yourself of past successes. Find a memory of sometime in the past when you have called someone or visited someone, a cold call of some kind, and it worked out very well for you.

Making cold calls on the phone is not my favorite thing. One of the techniques that I have used effectively was to put a photograph of one of my good clients right next to the phone. Whenever I was hesitant to make a call I would look at that photograph and it would remind me that I acquired that client by making a cold call on the phone. It made it easier to prevent the negative thoughts from entering my mind.

A third strategy is to remind yourself of future rewards. These would some specific thing that you will enjoy as a result of successfully completing this task. Tell yourself, "Well, if I can make a couple of appointments here, that will lead to engagements with decision-makers, that will lead to opportunities, that will lead to customers, that will lead to sales, that will lead to partnerships success and money. It's all ahead of me, all I need to do is complete this task." So you focus on future rewards.

Finally, act as soon as possible. The quicker you move into action and actually do something, the easier it is to move beyond that hesitancy or that fear that you have.

Effectively acquiring appointments is a core sales skill. If you cannot engage your prospects and customers in meaningful conversations, you cannot sell. Like every sales skill, it takes preparation, thoughtfulness, and the personal discipline to adhere to the best practices.

Terms

pre-call touch – some communication to the person that you want to talk to that is designed to make that person more receptive to your call.

pre-heat letter – a letter from someone else, to the person who you want to see, introducing you.

gatekeeper – someone whose job it is to open the door and allow access to someone, or to close the door, preventing you from

4. Acquiring Appointments

taking to the person you have targeted.

voice mail – a recording asking you to record a message to the person whom you are calling.

influencer – an individual within an account who can influence, but not make, the decision to purchase your product or service.

objection – a reason given to you by a prospect or customer which explains why he/she is not saying Yes.

script – a word-for-word, written presentation.

FIVE

5. Making a Sales Call Part I

Objective

In this chapter, we're going to begin to examine the heart of your job – making sales calls. Over the next four chapters, we'll explore the science of an effective sales call. Our objective is to equip you with the principles and process you need to master this most important part of your job.

We are assuming that you will be making a sales call on a prospect. As you recall, a prospect is someone who has not yet purchased something from you, so you haven't yet turned him/her into a customer. Many of the techniques and concepts that we discuss relative to making calls on prospects will also apply to customer calls. So, learning how to make an effective call on a prospect will equip you to be effective with customers as well.

Objectives of the sales call

Let's begin, with considering the purpose of the call. When you call on a prospect, the purpose isn't necessarily to sell something in the first call. It's great if you can, but generally that is not going to happen. That's an unrealistic expectation.

Instead, there are four different objectives for the first call.

Your first objective is to educate the prospect about your company and your company's solutions.

Your second objective is to acquire information about the person and the company on whom you are calling. Ideally, you'll identify opportunities, you'll quantify the potential of this account, and you'll understand this prospect's buying procedures and buying system.

The third objective is to personally relate to the customer, or more precisely, to help the customer personally relate to you. You want to begin to build a relationship, to establish a basis for your customer to become comfortable with you, and to see you as a competent person he or she can trust.

Finally, the fourth objective is to agree on a specific next step. You'll want to end your meeting with an agreement with the prospect for the next thing you are both going to do as a result of this time you spent together.

A successful first call on a prospect is defined by the extent to which you accomplish all four of these objectives. Ideally, you'll leave the sales call with your prospect knowing something about you, and with you gaining new knowledge of the prospect. You will have created the start of a relationship and you will have a specific agreement. That's an effective first sales call.

It's important to keep in mind that rarely do you attain 100% of these objectives. It's not an all or nothing situation. Success in each of

5. Making a Sales Call Part I

these issues is a matter of degrees. For example, it isn't necessarily that you either educate them or you don't. In all likelihood, there are different degrees to which you educate them. It's not that you learn something or you don't. It's that you acquire different degrees of knowledge. In each of these different objectives of a first sales call, there are degrees of effectiveness.

Here's a way of understanding this. Imagine a target for a dart game. It's perfectly round and formed by circles within circles. If you were to divide that target into quarters, you could label each quarter with one of the four objectives. One quarter could represent the objective of educating the prospect. One would represent the objective of learning about the prospect. One would represent the relationship portion and one would represent the agreement portion.

Now imagine the bull-eye portion of the target. In the middle is the bull's-eye, and there are rings and rings going around it. Each of those rings is a slightly greater distance away from the bull's-eye. As you get closer to the bull's-eye, to the center of the target, you're scoring more and you're collecting more points. As you get further away, towards the outer ring, you're less and less effective.

Ineffective

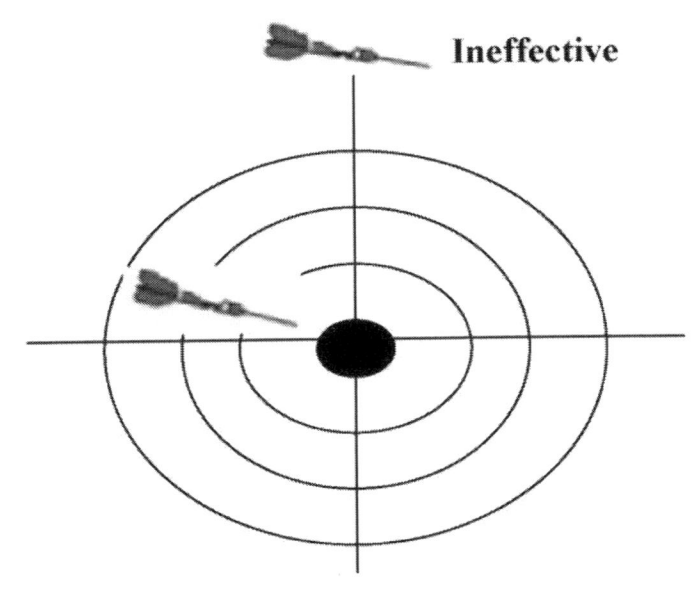

Let's now apply that illustration to our sales call. You can accomplish some things in each of these four quadrants that will be like sticking your dart in the bull's-eye. You can also score when you hit the outer rings of the target. Those are accomplishments that are less than the ideal, but still worthwhile accomplishments. Rarely will you through all four darts into the bull's-eye, and rarely will you hit the ideal with each of the four objectives of your sales call.

For example, let's examine the objective of educating the customer about you and your company. Let's say in this first sales call you begin to educate your customer, but he/she interrupts and says, "I don't want to hear it. Just give me a brochure." So you slide over a brochure and he says, "Thanks." How thorough and effective of a job have you done in educating the customer? Not at all. If you were to rate yourself on that slice, you'd probably be way outside the target. In the next sales call, you get into a thorough discussion with the

5. Making a Sales Call Part I

prospect about your company. He or she is very interested, asks a number of questions, takes notes, and spends a good half hour or so going into detail about what your company and you can do for this particular prospect. Where would that be on the bull's-eye target? That's probably as ideal as you could ever expect in a first sales call. You'd be right in the middle of the bull's-eye.

For each of these four different purposes, there is an ideal resolution as well as a spectrum of degrees of success. Frankly, very few sales calls ever achieve four bull's-eyes. When one does, you should celebrate because you just achieved a terrific sales call. More likely, your accomplishments are going to be spread out over the target. That does not mean, however, that you stop throwing at the bull's-eye. You need to try, on every single sales call, to hit the bull's-eye.

How To...

Now that you understand the four objectives of a sales call, the question is, how do you organize a first sales call on a prospect in order to achieve those objectives?

I'd like to give you another image to keep in your mind as you think about this. Think about how baseball is played. Imagine a baseball diamond.

Making a First Sales Call

Match

Understand

Open

Agree

Get an audience with the right people.

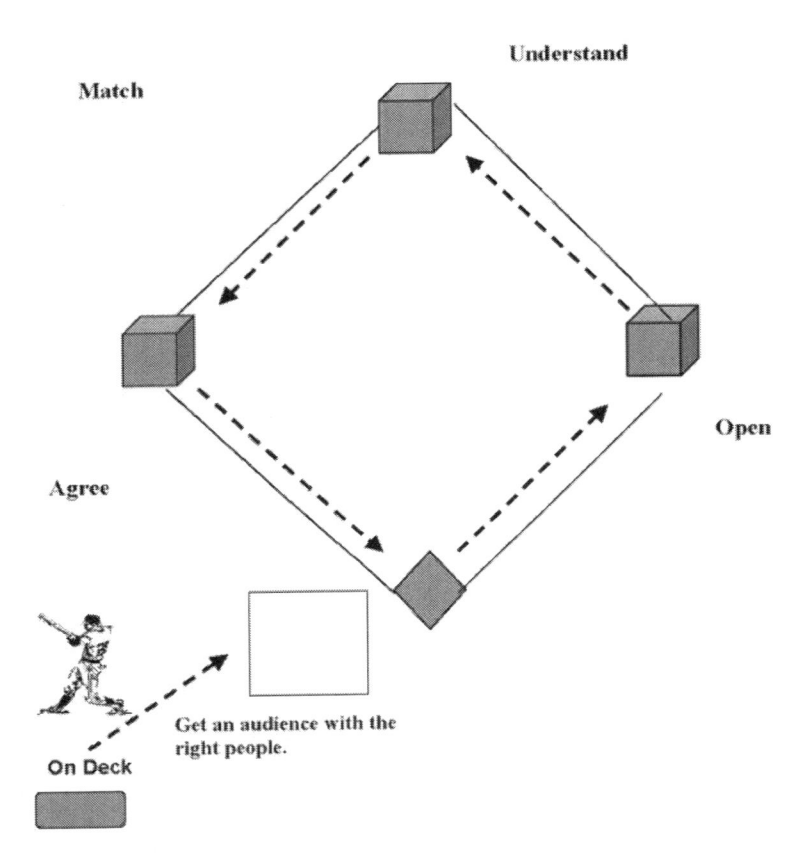

On Deck

Imagine looking at a baseball diamond from up above. What do you see on the ground? There's a circle off to the side of the batter's box. It's called the on deck circle. That's where the batter who is waiting to bat warms up and gets ready. Then you have the batter's box. Down the line is first base, then second base, third base and then home plate

That diagram is a way to visualize how to organize your first sales call. You start out in the on deck circle, then you progress to the batter's box, then first base, second base, third base, and home.

5. Making a Sales Call Part I

When you're in the on deck circle, you're just getting ready. You're really not in the game yet; you must get to the batter's box before you're in the game. So to, in a sales call, when you move from outside to gaining an audience with the "right people", you move from the on deck circle to the batter's box. If you never engage the "right people" you are like a batter who never got a chance to bat. You must first gain an audience with the right people, or you never get into the game. So the first step is to gain an audience with the "right people".

Now that you're up at bat, your next step is to hit the ball and run to first base. First base, when it comes to a sales call, means creating some openness to you and your company in the people with whom you are talking.

There are a couple different ways you can do that. You can create interest in yourself personally. The personal relationship (or first impression) that you are able to create in those first few moments may be enough to stimulate that prospect to be open to you. It's more likely, however, that they become interested in your company and what it has to offer. Either way, your job is to create an openness in them to listen to you, to interact with you, and to exchange information with you. When you do that, you've made it to first base.

Now that they are somewhat receptive and you've successfully made it to first base, you next must gain second base. That means that you learn about them. You find out what they want. You discover what products they're using, you find out how they're using them, you find out why they're using them, you find out what their business goals are. In short, you discover as much as you can about the prospect. When you understand the prospect, you've made it to second base.

Going from the batter's box to first base is a matter of opening, going from first base to second base is a matter of understanding. Now that you understand, you're on second base.

What happens if you're in a baseball game and you're on second base? You run to third, right? In order to go from second to third in a sales call you must present to the prospect something, some product, some service, or some possibility that matches what they want. You must educate them on something your company has that matches your best understanding of their need. That's why you must first spend the time understanding them. In baseball, you go from first base to second base; you don't go from first base to third. In a sales call, you must understand the customer before you can accurately present something to them.

In baseball, if you have managed to make it to third base, how many runs have you scored? None, because you haven't gotten home yet. A baseball player doesn't score until he crosses home plate. So it is with a sales call. You don't score until you get across home plate. That means that you come to some agreement with the prospect. The sales call culminates in an agreement of some kind.

That's the outline for how to achieve those four purposes we talked about. You open, you understand, you match, and you agree. You run the bases in every sales call.

5. Making a Sales Call Part I

Terms

educate – to teach the prospect/customer something. To instill some knowledge in the customer.

learn – to acquire some information about the prospect/customer that you did not have before.

relate – to create a sense of commonality with you, personally, in the prospect/customer.

agree – to have the prospect/ customer commit to some action he/she will take as a result of your interaction with him/her.

open – to create a sense of openness in the prospect/customer so that he/she will listen to what you have to say.

understand – to strive to learn about the important things about the prospect/customer.

match – to choose the features and benefits of your offer that most closely fit the needs and interests of the prospect/customer.

SIX

6. Making Your First Sales Call Part II

Objective

In the previous chapter we presented an overview of a first sales call on a prospect. We identified four objectives: to educate, to learn, to create a relationship, and to agree. You open, you understand, you match, and you agree after you've gotten an audience with the "right people". We also observed that there are different degrees of success in achieving each of those objectives in a sales call.

In this chapter, we're going to look at each of those areas and go into some more detail with specific suggestions about how to accomplish each of these.

The starting point

The first and most basic step is to begin by thinking about your prospect. Try to crawl into the mind and the heart of your prospect and see the world through his/her eyes. This is an essential process for a salesperson. If you are going to be at all effective, you must try to understand, relate and empathize with your prospect. This is not an event, it's not a step in the process, it is a constant habit that permeates everything you do.

A few years ago, a national organization of sales trainers conducted a study in which they tried to identify the characteristics of the best sales people in this country. They didn't want to study the good ones, they only wanted to study the very best, the cream of the crop, the absolute top. They identified the top five percent performers in a number of different industries and then studied them to see if they had anything in common.

Interestingly, they discovered a number of characteristics that the very best sales people had in common. The number one characteristic is this: "the ability to see the situation from the customer's point of view." That's it -- the outstanding characteristic of the best sales people.

What is encouraging about the conclusion is this -- we can learn to "see the situation from the customer's point of view." No one is born with the ability to see things from the customer's point of view – it is a learned behavior. And since it is a learned behavior, we can all learn to do it. Not only can we learn to do it, but we can continually learn to do it better and better. No matter how good you think you are at seeing the situation from the customer's point of view, you can improve.

So we're going to begin by thinking about your prospect, and trying to crawl into his or her mind, his or her heart, and see it from his or her situation. What is on your prospect's mind when you visit for the first time? Here's a list of questions that your prospect is thinking, either consciously or subconsciously, during your visit

- Why should I see you?

6. Making Your First Sales Call Part II

- Why should I listen to you?
- What do you think my problem is?
- How do you think it can be solved?
- Why should I trust you?
- Why should I trust your company?
- Why is your solution the best?
- Why should I take some action?
- Why should I do it now?"

Those are all questions bouncing around in the mind of your prospect.

Making it to first base

With that as perspective, let's apply our baseball analogy. Let's assume that you are in front of the "right people" – you've made it to the batter's box -- and now your job is to go to first base. In other words, to create some openness. What would be an ideal outcome of this part of the process? Ideally, if you hit the bull's-eye on this issue your prospect would be very open, would be very interactive with you, and would share a lot of information. That's the ideal for which to strive.

On the other hand, if you are out on the surface of the target, your prospect may not talk at all, shares nothing, and maybe gives you a perfunctory ten minutes before escorting you out.

How do you create openness? Start by focusing on the first impression. You only have one chance to make a good first impression and first impressions are incredibly important. Your prospect likely forms a judgment about you in the first thirty seconds of that interaction between you and your prospect. From then on, you are either reinforcing that impression or you're trying to change that impression. He or she begins with an impression, so you must make a good first impression when your prospect initially lays eyes on you. That's when you begin to build a relationship and create openness.

How do you do it? First, look as attractive as you can. Work with what you have. Your hair should be combed, your clothes neat and clean and your posture should project confidence. Smile a sincere smile. What happens when you smile at somebody? What do they do? Frown back? No. They smile back. Remember, you're beginning to build a relationship and create openness here.

There's always a question about clothes. How should you dress? Here's a rule that will serve you very well. Dress like your customer, only a little bit better. So in other words, if you are calling on farmers in the field, it's OK to wear boots and jeans and flannel shirts, but they better be clean, neat, and pressed, and a little bit better than your customer is wearing. If you're calling on a CEO in his office, you better be wearing a nice looking suit. If you're calling on a manager on a production line, it's OK to not have a tie. You just dress like your customer, only a little bit better, a step up. Don't allow clothes to separate you from your prospect. Instead make them a means of making a contact, a connection with them.

6. Making Your First Sales Call Part II

Secondly, your tone of voice should be as warm, real and personal as possible. Don't be too polished. Don't be aloof and professional, instead be real and warm. Make a sincere contact with real eye contact and a firm handshake. Your attitude should be confident, real and warm.

Don't forget the automobile that you drive. I cannot tell you how many times I've gone into to see a prospect and he or she said, "I watched you drive in." You don't know who's looking out that window at you. If you got a dirty car that hasn't seen the car wash in months, and if you get out and you look flustered, unorganized and intimidated, you may be making a horrible first impression and not even be aware of it. That first impression begins when you drive in to your prospect's place of business, so make sure that your automobile and your personal presentation are as powerful and positive as possible.

Introducing yourself and your company

At some point in the sales call, you'll need to introduce yourself and your company. To do this effectively, you should have created and memorized three different versions of an introduction.

The first should be just a few words. In those few words, you should explain to the prospect why he or she should be interested in you and your company. That takes some preparation so that it comes out as strong and attractive as possible. Prepare a script. Imagine that you can only say ten or 20 words to this person, and as a result, he or she will decide whether or not to spend any time with you. What are the most powerful 10-to-20 words you could say?

When you have that version ready, expand it to a few sentences. If you have thirty seconds to get a few sentences out, what would you say in those few sentences? The answer to that should be an introduction of maybe 200 to 250 words.

Finally, prepare a longer version for that person who is willing to listen. Fill a page with a well thought out answer to these questions: Who are you? What do you do? Why should your prospect care?

When you create three versions of that script, you'll have acquired a powerful tool to help make a positive first impression and create openness in your prospect.

Creating rapport

Next, focus on creating some rapport with the customer. That means making people comfortable with you. Your prospect is not going to want to spend time with you if he or she is not comfortable with you.

How do you make people comfortable with you? Number one, show interest in them. That's the implication of the law of reciprocity. The law of reciprocity is a very useful observation about human behavior. It's says people react to you the way you first act to them. If you're interested in them, they will, in turn, be interested in you. That's one of the most powerful laws of human behavior for a salesperson. Look around the prospect's environment. If you're meeting them in the office, study the décor of the office, or if you're meeting in a production area, look around the environment and find something to be interested

6. Making Your First Sales Call Part II

in. Look at them, the human being that's sitting there or standing across from you, and see if there are some expressions of that person's personality in their personal appearance.

Here's an example. I met a prospect for the first time. As I reached out and shook hands with him, I noticed he had a big turquoise and silver watchband. On his other hand was a big turquoise and silver ring, a great big ring. There's a story there. This is an expression of this person's personality. My goal was to create rapport by remarking on that, showing interest on that aspect of him or her. So I showed some interest in the turquoise and silver jewelry. You can do the same.

Another way to create rapport is to find common ground as quickly as possible. In the first few moments of your interaction with this prospect, search for something the two of you have in common. Sometimes it takes a little discipline to find those things.

Here's an example of what I mean by finding common ground. At the beginning of a first call on a prospect, the prospect asked me if I would like a cup of coffee. By the way, I always say, "Yes. I'd like a cup of coffee." Even if I just come from a breakfast meeting and I've had eight cups of coffee, and I'm beginning to perspire and wonder where the men's room is, I'm still going to say, "Ok. I'll have a cup of coffee." The reason for that is because he or she must then arrange for it. Sometimes he will go out and get it personally, and sometimes he will ask someone to get it. While the prospect is attending to the coffee, it gives me a few moments to look around to find something to be interested in.

In this case, when the prospect said, "Would you like a cup of coffee?" I said, "Sure." Off he went. I looked around and saw something that I could show interest in and to which I could relate. He had a very large picture of a sailboat hanging on his wall. As he came in and handed me the coffee I pointed to the sailboat on the wall and I said, "You sail, huh?"

He said, "Yes. That's my boat." The picture was so big I could see the name of the boat. Here's where it really got spooky because I said, "Ah. That's your boat?" He said, "Yes." I said, "Kelly Ann." That was the name of the boat. I said, "Kelly Ann? That's the name of the boat?" He said, "Yes." I said, "I have a daughter named Kelly Ann." He said, "So do I." We immediately found a connection. Not only did we both sail, we both had daughters, in fact with the same name.

You can imagine what happened there. We found common ground, we created a connection between two people, and he became very comfortable with me. That had nothing to do with selling anything. It did serve, however, to create some rapport, to make this person comfortable with me. In so doing, I was able to create openness in him, so that he would be receptive to what I had to say.

Suggestion number three for creating rapport is this: Reveal yourself as an individual. By that I mean find something that is unique and personal about yourself, and share it with your prospect as early in the conversation as you can. I know that goes against a lot of the common wisdom, but it's a powerful and effective technique for

6. Making Your First Sales Call Part II

creating openness. When you reveal yourself as a human being, as somebody with flaws and uniqueness, you create an understanding between your prospect and yourself that you are not just "a salesperson", not a stereotype; you're a real person.

Here's an example. Sometime, in the first few moments of a conversation with a prospect, I will work hard to find a way to interject into the conversation that my wife and I have been foster parents and over the years we have had nineteen foster children. What has that to do with sales? Nothing. What does it have to do with this human being on the other side of the desk seeing me as an individual? Everything. I have just broken that invisible wall that separates him or her and me. I have just smashed it apart because I have revealed myself as a human being. He can no longer treat me like a stereotype, a salesperson, because I have revealed myself as a human being.

Those are three different ways to create rapport, to make your customer comfortable with you, so that he or she will be open. When you have done that, you have opened the customer, and you have made it to first base. They're comfortable with you. They're ready to talk to you.

Making it to second base

Making it to second base means that you understand the customer sufficiently to allow you to present your products or services in a way that will be attractive to him. You understand the big picture within this account, and you also understand the specifics; you understand a specific opportunity for you.

Just like the other key objectives, there are levels of success to this one. You achieve success on the outer layer of the target when you walk away with just a superficial understanding. Maybe he or she handed you a brochure and said, "Here's who we are. Now leave us alone." In that case, you have not understood very well at all.

At the other end of the spectrum is the bull's-eye. You hit the bull's-eye when you have understood a great deal about the company and have identified a very specific opportunity. Obviously, like with the other objectives, there are degrees to success, and most of your sales calls will fall somewhere between these two extremes.

How do you understand a customer? You ask, you listen, and you observe. You try to organize this sales call so that seventy-five percent of the time the prospect is talking and you are talking only twenty-five percent of the time. If you can do that, you've will have the raw material for an excellent sales call.

Your primary tool for understanding the customer is a good sales question. You need to create a number of effective questions. That means that you prepare your major questions, word for word.

This is where the account profile that we discussed in a previous chapter will come in handy. You need to think through every type of customer and prepare, word for word, some questions that you can ask to help understand that person. The profile is a place to capture the answers to the questions.

I recall one of my seminar participants doing an excellent job

6. Making Your First Sales Call Part II

with question preparation. He created a three-ring b
right-hand side of the binder was a yellow pad where ̖
On the left-hand side there were several plastic sleeves, and
each sleeve was a piece of paper containing a list of questions for u
particular type of sales call. He could, therefore, sit in front of a prospect, open up his binder, take notes, and look at the questions on the left side and ask those questions in the sequence he had them, word for word, exactly the way he had prepared them. That's a great example of professional preparation.

There are different questions for different kinds of customers. You would ask different questions, for example, if you were calling on a truck line than those that you would ask if you were calling on a school system

Here are some good general questions that you can customize to the type of organization you may be calling on. These are particularly appropriate for a first call on a prospect.

1. "Tell me about your business." This is an open-ended question, which gives you some basic information.

2. "What do you know about my company?" This tells you if the prospect has had some previous experience, positive or negative, with your company.

3. "What is your role in the organization?" This question helps you to understand the individual and his or her position.

4. "What characteristics do you like in a supplier?" The answer to

this question gives you an understanding of the things that they feel are important.

5. "Can you give me a feel for which of our…" categories of product or services or whatever, you fill in the blank, "…you're currently using." The answer to this question provides you an understanding of their needs and a sense of their processes.

6. "What would make you consider us as a resource?" Or a different way of saying it, "What would have to happen for you to consider us as a resource?" Either of those kinds of questions gets you a feel for where that prospect is coming from.

7. "How are decisions made here?" Or a variation of that, "Who beside yourself is involved in the decision?"

8. "What opportunities do you have coming up that we might be involved in?" When they tell you about an opportunity, then you can begin to dig in to that and further understand that particular opportunity.

Just as there are some good questions to ask, there are also some types of questions, which you should not ask. Here are five types of questions to avoid.

Questions to avoid

1. Don't ask confrontational questions. They put the other person on the spot and make the other person defensive or make them look bad. That's one of the reasons why I never ask, "What do

6. Making Your First Sales Call Part II

you not like about your current supplier?" Who do you think chose the current supplier? Who do you think deals with the current supplier? If you ask this person to say what they don't like about them, more or less you're saying, "Tell me about the mistakes you've made." I don't think you're going to get a good answer. That's a confrontational kind of question. Don't ask that kind.

2. Don't ask trick questions. Buyers these days are much more sophisticated than ever. Don't try to artificially trick a person into a position. When you do that, you cause the other person to be suspicious of you.

3. Don't ask questions which are too personal. This is an issue that's relative to the degree of relationship that you have with the person. If you have known the person for years, you probably have built a close relationship, and you have earned the right to ask more personal questions. But on the first sales call, you should be careful about questions that are too personal.

4. Don't ask questions that are "put down" questions. Those are questions, which attempt to make another person look bad, or attempt to show that someone else doesn't know something. That's not the kind of thing you want to do when you begin a relationship.

5. Finally, don't ask questions that reflect some intense feeling.

You might be very, very frustrated with the way the call is going or frustrated with the other person, but don't try to put that all in a question that carries a lot of emotion to it. Remember, your job here is to understand.

Earlier, I indicated that when it comes to understanding your prospect, there are basically three methods: ask, listen, and observe. We've discussed asking, so now let's talk about listening and observing.

Listening

Why is it important to listen? Because when your customer talks, he/she gives you the material you need to sell him or her. Remember you can't get to third base unless you go to second base first. It's not enough to get your prospect talking, you must also then absorb the information your prospect shares. That means that you must listen.

Here are two techniques for listening well. First, concentrate on what the prospect is saying and not on what you want to say next. Try to force yourself to not think about what you're going to say next, rather concentrate on focusing on the prospect and what he or she is saying. One way to do this is to force yourself to concentrate by asking a question about what the prospect has just said. For example, let's say that you ask a question like, "Where is this business headed over the next few years?" The customer says, "Oh, we are really excited. We've got great growth plans." You might ask, "Oh. What kind of plans?" What you did was ask a question about what your prospect

6. Making Your First Sales Call Part II

said. When you get into that habit it forces you to concentrate on what your prospect is saying.

Another good technique to help you to concentrate is to repeat or paraphrase what he or she has said and give it back to them. Let's examine the same example. The prospect says, "Oh. We're real excited. We've got great growth plans and we've got all kinds of things happening. We're just so excited." You say, "Oh. So, in other words, you're really enthusiastic about the plans this company has." The prospect says, "Yes. That's right." What have you done? You just repackaged and repeated what he or she has said to you.

That's a very powerful listening technique because it forces you to think about what the prospect is saying. In addition, it communicates to him or her that you are, in fact, listening and striving to understand. That's a very powerful message to send. Deep at heart, when all of us are in a buying situation, one of the things we want from the people who are selling to us is for them to understand us. We want to be understood. If you can communicate to your prospect that you understand, you have gone a great distance forward in turning this prospect into a customer.

Observing

Finally, train yourself to observe. That means that you focus on this prospect from the moment you first spot their facility to the moment you leave. Take in all of the details. For example, one of my clients makes a point of noticing how many new cars are in the employee parking lot, because that gives them a sense of how successful this company is.

Other people focus on things like the cleanliness and organization of the building. If you're going back through a production line, notice the quality and the maintenance of the equipment. Notice the attitudes on the people as you interview this particular prospect. Observe everything you can. As you do, you gain an understanding of the customer.

Sometimes these understandings can be very helpful to you. I remember my very first sales position. I sold men's suits and sport coats in a relatively expensive men's store. I remember my boss, the manager of the store, training me. He said, "When someone comes back and is interested in a suit or a sport coat, I want you to observe their shoes." I said, "What?" He said, "Their shoes, because if someone wears expensive shoes and they take good care of their shoes, they will buy an expensive suit. If they wear cheap, poorly kept shoes, they are not going to spend the money on an expensive suit." I thought, "Well, this guy probably knows more about it than I do." So I trained myself to observe people's shoes when they came in to look at a suit and then steer them accordingly. Good shoes, expensive suits: inexpensive shoes, cheap suits. It turned out to be a very helpful observation.

Terms

script – a verbal presentation which is prepared, word-for-word, in writing, and practiced prior to be presented.

6. Making Your First Sales Call Part II

rapport – the feeling in the prospect/customer that you are like him/her: a sense, on the part of the prospect/customer that you have things in common.

GSQ – acronym for Good Sales Question

observe – the process of learning important things about a prospect/customer by noticing indications in the prospect/customer's physical plant, and in the demeanor and comments of the prospect/customer's employees.

SEVEN

7. Your First Sales Call Part II

Objective

In this chapter, we're going to continue our analysis of your first sales call, looking at one more aspect of that call.

As you recall, there are four objectives for this first sales call. First is to educate the prospect about your company and some of the products and services available. Second is to learn about the interests, the needs and the dynamics of the account. The third objective is to begin the process of building a relationship with the customer. The fourth objective is to come to some kind of an agreement on the next step.

In the last couple of chapters, we discussed how to organize to achieve these objectives by using the baseball diamond as an easy to remember analogy. You go from an on deck circle to the batter's box by getting an audience with the "right people". You go from the batter's box to first base by creating openness -- rapport and comfort on the part of your customer. You go from first base to second base by understanding what your customer is all about, their needs, their interests, their desires, their wants, etc. Now it's time to go from second base to third base.

Making it to third base

You move from second base to third base by matching your products or services to the prospect's needs, and then presenting that proposal. This falls under the heading of educating your customer in a very special way. Let's begin with some terms. The first is "match". That's not something that you start a fire with. When we talk about it in this context, it means that you select the elements of your company, of your product, of your service, and of yourself that most accurately meet your customer's needs and appeal to his or her interests.

There are hundreds of different things that you could you talk about relative to your company, yourself and your products. In the seminars that I teach on this, we often do an exercise in features and benefits. I'll ask the seminar participants to list features of their company. They can always come up, when they are prodded and challenged, with literally hundreds of different things to talk about. The problem with that is that you cannot possibly talk about everything there is. You cannot possibly educate your customer to all the things that he or she could know about you, your company and your product. You have to select the most important aspects of your company, yourself, your product, your service. Secondly, what is important to one customer may not be important to another. So, you must select those that most accurately meet each individual customer's needs. That's the criteria you use to decide what to talk about. So the word "match" means that you select the appropriate elements that you want to present.

7. Your First Sales Call Part II

The second word is "proposal". A "proposal" is an offer that you make. It's an offer to your prospect to buy or to take some action, which leads to a sale. For example, you might show a product, talk about it and provide a price quote for it. Your offer is, "Buy this product." That's a proposal. Or you might say, in regards to a product you are showing, "The next step is to meet with your engineer or your department manager." Your proposal is to meet with the engineer. It is not to buy the product, it's to take the next step towards buying the product. The proposal is the action that you suggest to your prospect.

Presenting is the act of making your proposal. Your proposal is the offer you make, the content of what you are suggesting. Presenting is the act of making that proposal.

Moving from second base to third base, then, involves presenting a proposal that matches the prospect's needs.

Let's go back to the image of a target with a bull's-eye. There are different levels of success when you engage in this particular step in the sales process. When you hit the bull's-eye, you present a product or a service and you ask the customer to buy that.

However, most of the time you will present an offer to take the next step. For example, at one time I sold surgical staplers. That was a long and involved sale. I first needed to see the hospital purchasing agent and obtain his/her permission to be in the hospital. In the hospital, I had to see the operating room supervisor and gain her permission to be in the operating room suite. Then I had to get into the surgeons locker room and change into hospital greens so that I looked like a surgeon. At that point, I finally had an opportunity to approach the surgeon. I'd show him the staplers and then ask for the next step, which was to get into the surgical suite itself so that I could be with him when he used our instruments for the first time.

I didn't get a chance to really ask for the order, the purchase of the product, until I was in the operating room with the surgeon. Everything else was a step towards that. In terms of hitting the bull's-eye, I didn't even have a chance to hit the bull's-eye until I was in the operating room with the surgeon. All of the others were steps towards that purchase. They landed on the larger, outer rings of the bull's-eye.

So it is with what you sell. Often it is not appropriate to ask for a purchase because it's just not the right thing to do. What is the right thing to do is to ask for the next step. When you make a proposal, sometimes you make a proposal to purchase the product; sometimes you make a proposal for the next step. You hit the bull's-eye by asking your prospect to purchase; you achieve the mid-layer of the target when your proposal is for the next step. You remain on the outer ring if you can't find anything else, so you propose to the prospect that the two of you get together again at a later date. When he or she agrees to see you again, you're at the outer ring of the bull's-eye.

How well you do this, how close you come to hitting the bull's-eye with this stage of the sales process, depends on how well you accomplish the earlier parts of the sales process; how well you understand the customer, how well you relate to them, and how well you learn about them.

7. Your First Sales Call Part II

You are going to present a proposal that matches what you understand the prospect's needs to be. So you must prepare for that. At some point in the future, you will be able to some of this on the spur of the moment. But now, at this stage in your progress on the job, you probably don't have sufficient product knowledge to do that. Rather, you should begin by preparing presentations of two or three products.

Work with your manager to select those items that your manager feels, from his or her experience, will be those that are most likely to be received warmly and will most likely match the needs of the people you are going to see.

Having selected a couple of products or services that you're going to focus on for your first round of sales calls, you next need to prepare presentations for each of those products.

When you prepare a presentation, think in terms of preparing a menu of different items. You will not present all of these items to every person, but you will select from the menu a different combination for each individual. Your menu contains a list of features and benefits about the product that you're selling.

Understanding features and benefits

Let's define these terms. A feature is a describable characteristic of the thing that you're selling. For example, let's say that right now you're sitting there reading this book and you're using a mechanical pencil to take notes. Look at that pencil a moment. What are some of the describable characteristics of the pencil? It might have a button at the top, such that when you press it, it advances the lead. The push button is a describable characteristic of the pencil – a feature. It might be made out plastic, it might weigh a certain amount, it might be shaped a certain way, and it might be made in a certain country. It might have printing on it that has some kind of message. All those are features; they are describable characteristics.

What are some of the other features of this pencil? The cost of the pencil; the way it's purchased. Do you purchase it over the Internet? Do you call a toll free number? How do you purchase it? In what quantity? What are the shipping arrangements? All of those are characteristics of the pencil.

Create a menu of features. Visualize a column with features of the product that you're focusing on, listed from top to bottom in the column. Then think of a column next to that. In that next column you're going to take each feature and turn it into a benefit.

What's a benefit? A benefit is a statement of what this feature means to the customer. When you talk about a feature you talk about the thing that you're selling. However, when you talk about a benefit, you talk about the person to whom you're selling. There's a nice phrase that you can use to make the transition: "This means that you…" and then fill in the blank.

Let's go back to our mechanical pencil. You're showing someone this pencil and you say, "It has a button at the top. When you push the button it projects the lead out a little bit. When you keep the button pushed down and push the lead onto the table or the desk it

7. Your First Sales Call Part II

pushes the lead back up." That's a feature; you've just talked about the thing. Now you need to translate that feature into a benefit -- a statement about the person. We just said, "and it pushes the lead back into the pencil." You turn that into a benefit by saying, "This means that you will never have to worry about lead soiling your shirt pocket or inadvertently marking on any papers that you're working on because the lead will be retracted." The feature is that the lead retracts and the benefit is that you don't have to worry.

When you translate a feature into a benefit, the subject of the sentence changes. When you're discussing the feature, the subject is the product you're selling. When you're discussing the benefit, the subject of the sentence is the person to whom you're selling it. Again, a feature describes the thing; a benefit describes the impact on the person.

Every feature has different benefits for different people. When you create a presentation you have a menu of features and benefits and then you select, you match, the appropriate features and the appropriate benefits for the person to whom you are selling. That's what a good presentation is all about. You need to keep in mind that every product that you sell is viewed differently, depending on the job title and the interest of the person to whom you're selling it.

Let me go back to this example from my days of selling hospital supplies. At one time, I sold surgical gloves. These are the gloves that the surgeons and nurses wore in surgery. Let's assume different people in the hospital have a part of the decision to buy a certain brand of gloves. If you're the purchasing agent and you're looking at the gloves, what are you interested in? What features or benefits are you interested in? Primarily, price and availability. You don't care how the glove feels. You don't care how it looks. You don't care what color the packaging is. You don't care about any of those things. You want to know is it priced right and can they get it with a minimum of concern and hassle. That's the concerns of a purchasing agent.

Let's say we go talk to the surgeon. Does the surgeon care about those things? Not a bit. The features he is interested in are the fit and the feel and the durability of the glove. Is it likely to tear in the middle of surgery? Is it comfortable to wear?

How about the nurse whose job it is to supply the operating room personnel during the course of a surgery? The circulating nurse's job is to get the materials from locations around the surgical field and to pass them to the sterile field whenever they are required. What is he or she concerned about? Is it the fit and feel? No. This person is concerned about being able to immediately tell the size and pick the right size without any mistakes. A color-coded size and big labels – those are the features that appeal to this person.

You see, then, that the features you choose to match depend on the individual to whom you are talking. A good presentation draws from an ala carte menu of features and benefits. You select the items that are most appropriate to that particular customer.

Once you create this ala carte menu, the next step in your preparation is to memorize it. What? Yes, memorize it. Why is that?

7. Your First Sales Call Part II

Because when you memorize each of these items, the words will come out of your mouth in a fairly powerful way. You're not going to try to make it up at the spur of the moment. You take the time to create the best words, in the most powerful way. You think it through and develop the most persuasive way to describe something. Then you memorize it so that those words come out pretty close to what you have prepared. When you memorize something that you prepare beforehand, your presentation is more powerful.

Secondly, you memorize these ala carte items on the menu because that frees you to focus on your prospect. Generally, when you're having a conversation with someone, and the other person is talking, what are you thinking about as you listen to the other person speak? More times than not, you're thinking about what you're going to say back. Suppose you already knew what you were going to say back. That would free you from thinking about it; it would free you to focus on what the other person was saying and what they were trying to communicate. You could be far more sensitive to the other person. Memorizing the features and benefits provides you that opportunity. You don't have to think about what you're going to say. You can focus on understanding your customer.

Your preparation, then, means that you create an ala carte menu of features and benefits, and memorize it. Then you prepare a proposal by selecting the items from your menu that you believe most closely match the prospect's needs. You prepare to explain those features and translate them into appropriate benefits for the person to whom you are presenting.

The next step is to create or gather appropriate audiovisual materials. Do you have literature that describes this? What about a sample? Do you have something other than just your words to help convey what this product or service does? That's part of your preparation

The final step of preparation is to prepare an appropriate next step. When it's not appropriate for the customer to say, "Yes. I'll buy some," when there's something else -- a different next step -- you should be able to have that next step firmly in your mind so that you can present it to the prospect. When you have selected the items from your ala carte menu of features and benefits, when you have them memorized, when you have your literature or your samples in hand, and when you have in mind both the proposal to buy it as well as the proposal for the next step, you are ready to educate the customer in this very important part of the sales process. Your preparation is finished.

During the sales call itself, when you sense that you have an understanding of this prospect's needs and interests and you are ready to present your proposal, you select those features and benefits that most closely match your understanding of the prospects needs and interests and you tell him or her about them using your audio/visual materials, using your samples, using your literature and presenting the most appropriate features and benefits to the prospect. That is what matching, moving from second base to third base, is all about.

When you've done that, you're ready to move on to the next

7. Your First Sales Call Part II

portion of the sales call.

Terms

match – to select the elements of your company, of your product, of your service, and of yourself that most accurately meet your customer's needs and appeal to his or her interests.

proposal – an offer that you make.

presenting – the act of making your proposal.

feature – a describable characteristic of the thing that you're selling.

benefit – a statement of what this feature means to the customer.

ala carte menu – a list of features and their corresponding benefits from which you select in order to make a presentation about a product, service or program.

EIGHT

8. Your First Sales Call Part III

Objective

In this chapter, we're going to focus on the process of coming to an agreement with the customer. That's the fourth objective for a sales call. In sales vernacular, we're going to call it "the close".

Let's put this in perspective. We're still working on understanding the dynamics of the first sales call on a prospect. We've identified the four purposes of this first call: to educate, to learn, to build a relationship, and to come to some agreement. We've discussed methods to employ to accomplish all of this.

In our analogy, we've moved from the on deck circle in our baseball diamond, all the way around to third base. At this point, how many runs have scored? None. Nothing really counts until you come across home plate. Coming across home plate and scoring a run is what happens when we gain some agreement with the prospect.

Closing

First of all, let's define what it means to close. A close is an agreement for action. Think of the capital letter A2 (Agreement for Action). When your prospect agrees to take some action, you have successfully closed that interaction.

Here's an example. Let's say that you talk to your prospect about a product or service. Your prospect says to you, "This looks really interesting. Will you send me some additional literature? I'd like to study this some more." You say, "Yes. Sure. I'd be happy to."

Have you closed? Have you an agreement for action? The answer is no. You've agreed to take some action; you will send him some additional information. What has your prospect agreed to do? Nothing. A close always involves an agreement for action on the part of your prospect. The person on the other side of the desk must agree to take some action, or you haven't closed.

Let's go back to our situation. He or she says, "Send me some literature will you?" You say, "Yes. I'd be happy to. If I send it to you and get it arrives here on Wednesday, can you and I have a telephone conversation about it Thursday?" If he or she says, "Yes," then he's agreed to take some action -- to talk with you about it. That's the next step. You've closed by getting an agreement for action.

Just like in all the other aspects of a sales call we've examined, there are degrees of success to closing. We can, again, use the target as a way to understand that. You hit the bull's eye when your prospect says, "Ok. I'll take it. Here's a purchase order."

It doesn't get much better than that, but you don't always hit the bull's-eye. More likely than that, you can still come to some agreement without necessarily being right at the center of the target.

You close when they agree to the next step, "Yes, I will see you

8. Your First Sales Call Part III

next week at ten o'clock" or "Yes. You can go see the department head. Let me call him or her." When you acquire that kind of an agreement, you've hid midway between the bull's-eye and the outer ring.

When they agree to nothing other than to see you again, you have gained an outer ring agreement. It's better than nothing.

You're completely off target; you've missed the whole thing if you come out of the sales call with absolutely no agreement at all.

How to

How do you go about this process of coming to some agreement for action? There are several rules for you to follow.

Rule number one is Always ask for action. It is very easy to leave a sales call without ever asking for some kind of an agreement. Instead, every time you see a customer or a prospect, every time you have a conversation, ask for an agreement for action. Most outside salespeople error on the side of rarely asking for action. Instead of doing it all the time, they do it rarely. As a result, projects and opportunities linger on and on and on and never get resolved. One of the reasons you always ask for action is to resolve the issue; to bring it to some kind of conclusion so that you can be free to move on. One of the biggest detriments to your effectiveness is the project that never gets resolved. It's not the "no" that's the problem. It's the "maybe" or "I don't know" that's the problem. When you ask for action, you bring the issue to resolution, and you clarify the next step.

Rule number two states: When you ask, make, sure it's an appropriate request. That means that you do not ask for something that is impossible or very difficult for the prospect to agree to. For example, let's say you're talking to the director of purchasing, and you've presented your green widget. There's an understanding that in order for this company to buy the green widget they have to get a department head to approve it and several production people to look at it and approve it also. In this situation, it would be very inappropriate for you to say, "Can I have a purchase order?" That request is inappropriate. It's not the next step. You're going to look foolish by asking for things that are inappropriate for this particular customer in this particular situation. So rule two states that you always make a request that is appropriate to the situation.

Rule three states: Use prepared closing questions. In other words, memorize and get very comfortable with three or four closing questions that you can use in almost any kind of situation, under any circumstances. There are a couple reasons for that. One reason is that the biggest obstacle to closing is within our own minds. We're hesitant to close because we know that this brings the issue to resolution and we're afraid to hear a "no". Since we are anxious about this, we have a tendency to avoid it. So we don't ask for action, and projects get lost in limbo and things go on forever and ever.

How do you overcome that mental obstacle to closing? One way to overcome it is to be thoroughly prepared. Preparation makes you confident, and when you're confident you're much more likely to do those things that you want to do. You need to prepare completely.

8. Your First Sales Call Part III

That's why you create, word for word, three or four closing questions that you personally are very comfortable with.

Than you practice saying them so that you're comfortable and confident and much more likely to actually voice those questions. Here are a couple of generic closing questions that you can ask to bring the issue to resolution.

You can say, "What's the next step?" That's an assumptive close because it assumes that there is a next step and it gives the opportunity to the prospect to define what to do next. Then he or she will say, "Well, the next step is to see the production manager about this." You say, "Ok. When can we do that?" He says, "Next Tuesday." You have an agreement. We'll see the production manager next Tuesday. That's an agreement. Good for you. You started the process by asking the question, "What's the next step?"

Here's another one, very similar, "Where do we go from here?" That's a nice easy, comfortable close. Notice that it assumes that we go. The two of us are going to do something together. You haven't asked the customer "if" we can go, you've asked him to identify "where" you go together.

Those are what I call generic closing questions. These are samples of a class of closing questions that you can develop which will be specific for your situation. Develop some closing questions word for word, practice them, and memorize them, so that when it comes time to ask for an agreement, to bring this issue to resolution, you will have words that come out of your mouth with which you are very ple.

Rule four states: Have some alternatives in mind. In other words, you're always going to ask for Plan A, but sometimes they're not going to say yes to Plan A. In that case you need to have an alternative for this prospect. You need to have Plan B ready. Here's an example. One of my clients was a CPA firm that wanted to increase their bookkeeping business. We created a system that generated leads. The CPAs would go out and see prospects who were interested in the possibility of giving them their bookkeeping business.

After their presentation, they asked for an agreement, "Can we be your bookkeeper?" Often the prospect wasn't ready to say yes to them at that point. The prospect would often voice some kind of delay or objection. At that point, the accountants were taught to ask for Plan B. They would say, "Ok. I can appreciate that you're not quite ready for that. Let me suggest this; How about if you give us a copy of your financial statements and we'll analyze them and bring you a two page analysis of what we see about your company?" That wasn't an agreement for the business, but it was an appropriate alternative. If they said yes to Plan B, it kept the relationship alive and moving forward.

Rule five is Prepare responses to objections. Remember the work that you did when we created scripts to ask for an appointment. We described a process to think through that which you are likely to hear, and then to create an outline of how to respond when you hear that. It's a matter of preparation.

8. Your First Sales Call Part III

Suppose you close by saying, "Can I have a purchase order?" Now suppose that your prospect voices an objection or two. Your job is to know what you're going to say prior to them actually coming up with the objection. You need to prepare a response to those objections that you're most likely to hear.

Much of selling has to do with preparation. In the last chapter we talked about preparing your presentation and preparing your a la carte menu. In this session we're talking about preparing the language that you're going to use to ask questions and to prepare an alternative. Closing effectively demands that you prepare responses to objections that you're likely to hear so that you're not trying to come up with the most effective thing on the spur of the moment. Rather, you're taking time, when you have the time, to think it through, to put together a persuasive response and to practice it.

Reviewing the sales call

Let's review the entire sales call. We identified four objectives. Number one is to educate the prospect about your company, your products, your services and yourself. Number two is to learn about the prospect, to understand, and to gather information. The third objective is to begin the process of building a relationship with this human being, one human being with another. The fourth objective is to come to some agreement for action. Each of these are things that you should be attempting in every sales call.

Further, we discussed the concept of the bull's-eye target; that there are different degrees of success for each of these four objectives. If you hit the bull's-eye with every one of these, congratulations, but that hardly ever happens. Most often, your darts are thrown all over the target. That's true in a sales call as well.

We also used the analogy to the baseball diamond as an outline. If you gain an audience with the "right people" that gets you to the batter's box. When you create some openness in the customer that gets you to first base. You understand the customer, and that gets you to second base. You match your offering to your customer's needs, and that gets you to third. You gain an agreement with your customer for some action, and that gets you to home plate.

After the call

Now you've finished the sales call. Congratulations. As you do more and more of these you'll get better at it. Right now, you're not quite finished yet. You need to record some of the details. So when you walk out to your automobile and sit down, don't start it and immediately drive to your next call. Rather, take a moment and make notes about what happened. Take out that account profile that we talked about and complete that as best you can. Fill in the missing blanks on your personal profile. Make notes in the contact log about what went on in this sales call. What's going to happen next time? What should you do next time? Then if there are any things that developed that you need to take care of put those on your to-do list. Now you're ready to move on to the next sales call.

8. Your First Sales Call Part III

Terms

close – an agreement for action. It must involve your prospect/customer agreeing to do something that moves the project forward.

A2 – The symbol for Agreement for Action, the definition of a close.

A3 – Always Ask for Action, the first rule for closing.

objection – a stated reason, on the part of the prospect/customer, to not say yes.

NINE

9. Developing Account Strategies

Objective

Our objective for this chapter is to equip you with an understanding of the principles and processes you'll need in order to develop effective account strategies.

Keep in mind that you are in it (this job) for the long-term. This is not a six-month job. You're going to be doing this work, calling on these customers and developing this business for some time. Rarely will you make one sales call on someone and then never see them again. More likely, you will come to know these customers. You can't expect to sell everything to everyone on the first call. That means you will see them again and again and again. That means that you must view each of your customers from that long-term perspective.

Not all accounts are alike. They are different in their needs, in the dynamics of each situation, in the personalities of the people and the competitive situation that they present. Every account that you call on is somewhat different from all others. That means that you cannot treat each one the same.

Add these two observations together, and it means that you must create an individual long-term strategy for each account to whom you sell.

First, let's define our terms. Strategy means a series of steps designed to bring your prospect or customer from where they are now to where you want them to be. It's the long-term view. Realistically, it's a planned series of sales calls in which each sales call has a distinctive set of purposes, a distinctive piece of education, a person or set of people to speak with, and a distinctive agreement that you'd like to attain. The purpose, the timing, the organization, and the sequence of that series of sales calls is the strategy. It's the long-term perspective, the big picture, of what you want to do and how you want to do it.

It's like a football game. In every football game the coach develops a game plan. That plan describes how he wants the team to go about each individual play, ending up in winning the game. The plays themselves are like sales calls. Sales calls are the tactics, but the big picture into which they fit is the strategy. It's the strategy, the big picture, that we'll focus on in this chapter.

First, let's review the two basic sales processes we examined in the first chapter. The first one focuses on creating customers, and the second one focuses on creating partners out of customers. You recall that the process works like this: first you identify suspects, and then you turn suspects into prospects, and prospects into customers. That's one set of sales calls. That's one strategy to achieve a purpose -- to influence someone to purchase from you for the first time.

Then the second part of the overall sales process is to take those customers, people who have purchased, turn them into clients,

9. Developing Account Strategies

and finally turn a client into a partner. In terms of the biggest, most basic strategy, you strive to turn every prospect into a partner.

Let's assume that you have made at least one sales call on a series of prospects. In the course of those first few sales calls, you have discovered some things about each of those prospects.

You have gained a sense for the situation at each account. Now you have to make some decisions. What do you do? What strategy do you follow to turn each prospect into a customer?

Here are some typical situations that you're likely to encounter. We'll describe each situation and then discuss an appropriate strategy.

Situation Number One:

Here's the first one. You visit a prospect for the first time and discovered that right now they have no opportunity for you. "You're a nice person. We like your company. We just don't have any opportunity for you at this moment." That's a very common discovery in a first sales call on a prospect. What do you do? What's your strategy?

You must get the prospect to agree on a reason to see you again. Each time that the prospect sees you again, you must try to create an opportunity by completing the first couple steps of the sales call in ever more detail. In other words, you must create an opportunity by understanding this prospect deeper and deeper. Then you methodically present your products to them, focusing on those that you believe most appropriately match their needs. Make sure that you present your most effective or most attractive product. Present that ace that you have that everyone has to buy from you because it's such a great value.

As you continue to call on them, you strive to extend your relationships into all parts of the account. If you have been working with the purchasing agent, try to see the operational people. When they see you, go back to that original sales call and do each of the steps deeper. Try to uncover an opportunity that they may not even be aware of. While it seems odd, it happens regularly. It is common to hear your first contact say, "No. Everything's fine. We don't have any needs. Our current vendors are taking care of us." But the situation often is different when you gain access to the production area or back where the operation takes place and you talk to some of those people. If you ask questions of them, you almost always find things that aren't quite right. If you can get to that level and dig to that depth you will discover some of those things, which you can turn into opportunities. If something is not quite right, that's an opportunity for you to fix it by presenting your product or service.

Situation Number Two:

What about the situation in which you have met with a prospect and there is an opportunity. What do you do now? What's the next step?

Try to turn every opportunity presented to you into two steps, particularly when you are new and meeting people for the first time. For example, they may say something like this, "Yes. We're interested in your blue widgets; there is a possibility of doing some blue widget business here."

At that point you can say, "OK. Well, my blue widgets are ten dollars a dozen. Do you want some?" You could present your solution and ask them to buy some.

I believe it is more effective in the long run to turn this opportunity into two sales calls. Don't just immediately say, "Well, here's our deal" and hope to close it then. I'd rather you create an opportunity to get back into this account two times. The first time you'll dig deeper to understand their situation deeper. The second time you'll present your best proposal.

So, I'd rather you say, "Ok. What I'd like to do is come back next week and talk with the people who are actually using the blue widgets and gain a better idea of that application, then after I do that I'll come back and present our widget solution.

Why would you do that? That doesn't sound very efficient. No, it's not efficient, but it's effective. Remember, you are in this for the long-term. You are building relationships. You are gaining trust. You are understanding the customer. If you can take this opportunity that they have presented to you, and turn it into an opportunity to meet more people, to understand this prospect deeper, and then to make a sharper, more focused, more perfectly matched proposal, in the long-term you're going to be much better off. You're going to have broadened and deepened your relationship in the account.

Consider, also the concept of an enticer. What's an enticer?

An enticer is a small purchase, an easy thing for your customer to buy that opens the door for you in that account. Once you have something that the account buys from you, you can take advantage of that relationship that you're building to expand to other types of business. Here's an example. I was working with a client company that repaired and serviced computer hardware. They really were not interested in you bringing a broken monitor to them to fix. What they really wanted to do was come into your business and write a service contract to maintain all of your equipment.

From the customer's perspective, that's a big risk and a substantial amount of money. Most people, on the basis of one sales call, were not really interested in giving that much responsibility to a company that they did not know that well. Understanding that, rather than ask for that contract initially, we created an enticer.

Remember, an enticer is an offer that is easy to say yes to, and that opens the door and gives you an opportunity to expand the business. The enticer we developed was this. When the salesperson offered their preventative maintenance service contract they would also say something like this, "Now I realize that you may not be ready for this big purchase, so what we'd like to do is just find some way that you can get to know us and we can get to know you a little better. Here's a coupon for 50 percent off the repair charge for your next piece of equipment. Anytime anything in here needs to be repaired, you can take this coupon and give it to us and we'll repair it for half of our normal cost. We're losing money on that, you understand that, but we're investing in you, the customer, and we think that if you will do this little piece of business with us, you'll get to know us and we'll get to know you, and then we'll have an opportunity to go further." They presented it just like that. It was an enticer -- an opportunity to come back in and reestablish and build the relationship.

The idea is if you get them buying something, it gives you a reason to be there and an opportunity to expand the business.

You may recognize an underlying strategy at work here. It is that you use every opportunity to expand the relationship, to know more people, to ingrain yourself deeper in every account. The two strategies we discussed, using an opportunity to expand the relationship and developing and enticer, are both variations on this core approach.

Situation Number Three:

What about the prospect who says, "We're very happy with our current vendor?"

What's your strategy in an account that's loyal to a competitor?

Two possibilities. First, don't compete. Don't go head to head with the competition. You'll lose. Instead, go around the competition. It is likely that the competitor is supplying a lot of the high volume, high visibility products and services in this account. That's why that competitor is visible and why there's some loyalty. At the same time, that vendor is probably not supplying everything. It is possible that this particular account is buying some things from someone other than the competitor. Those are the items on which you should focus. Don't

,e competitor head to head where he or she is strong.

after the little bits and pieces of business that might be currently eluding that competitor.

Take the business away from someone else – someone who is a smaller player in this account. Then, after you have gained some of these smaller pieces of business, you establish a presence in that account and you can begin to build on that basis. At some point, if you're successful, you may be positioned strongly enough in the account to go head up with your competitor later. The first strategy is to go around them, not through them.

The second strategy is to clearly and plainly present yourself as a second option. Say, "Yes I appreciate that the competitor is doing all the business and that's fine. Good for you. At some point in time you may want a backup supplier. It would be good for you to have a trusted secondary source." You position yourself as the secondary source, the Plan B in their eyes. As you do that, you again create a presence in the account. If you're successful in doing that, you provide the account a reason to see you again. Every time you are in that account you have an opportunity to push your agenda forward.

Situation Number Four:

What about the prospect that you just can't get anywhere with? They won't talk. They just won't give you any information. You don't know exactly what's going on. You don't know because the account doesn't talk much. What do you do?

9. Developing Account Strategies

This is the most difficult of all situations to work with. You must create some opportunity in this account. If you don't, nothing is going to happen. You can't sell effectively in an account that will not talk with you.

You must get past that. You have to have information. You must understand and learn about your prospect. The sales process is dependent on that. Until you get them talking, until you uncover some opportunity, until you get some information, you're going to be stymied.

There are a couple of things that you can do to get a non-communicative customer talking. One is to tell stories about other people. I don't mean gossip. Rather, tell success stories. Tell stories about other accounts that you believe are like this one. Tell stories about their needs and their applications and what they've done with some of the product categories that you sell. Then ask them, "Are you like that? Does any of that relate to you? Does any of that make sense to you?" You tell a story about someone else and then ask the customer or the prospect if they are like the person in this story.

Another way is to use open-ended questions. An open-ended question is a question for which there is no right or wrong, and one in which the customer must talk a bit and explain. For example, you could say, "Tell me about…" Use the words "tell me" and then fill in the blanks. Every time you use the words "tell me," you're asking an open-ended question that prompts the customer to speak a lot.

Another tactic is to verbally present them a list of items and ask them to respond to each list. Ask, "Do you have any needs for this?

Do you use any of that? What's your position in regards to this?" You methodically work down through your list, expecting to hear yes or no answers. And, as they give you those yes or no answers, you take notes and gain something of an understanding of this account.

Another strategy is to methodically present all of your most powerful products. Take one in at a time, present that one and ask for their reaction, their response. "Do you use anything like this? Does this make any sense to you?" You let them react to your presentation.

All of those are different tactics. Which works for which prospect? I don't know. You must work that out.

In every case you must get information from the account before you can do anything in that account. You must figure out a way to get a non-communicative customer or prospect talking and sharing information with you. With no information you cannot go any further. Information and conversation with your customer is the commodity that you work with as a professional salesperson.

In both of these last two situations; in the account that's in the hands of the competitor and the account that won't communicate with you, you need to objectively assess the potential of the account. In other words, is it worth putting a lot of time and effort in even if you gain all the business? It may be that your time is better spent elsewhere. It may be that their position is so hardened that it would take you three or four years to influence them to change that position. It may be that the potential payback isn't worth it.

9. Developing Account Strategies

It may be that it is worth it, but that's a question you need to ask about these last two kinds of situations. Is it worth it? Assess the potential. If you decide that it is worth it, then you do need to be persistent and understand that at eventually something will change.

I remember being very frustrated with one of my accounts that was a non-communicative customer in the hands of a competitor. I just couldn't get anywhere in that account. I expressed my frustrations to my manager. He gave me some very wise advice. He said, "Remember, the only thing that you can count on is that something will change. You don't know what and you don't know when but you know that it will, and your job is to position yourself to be the person they look to when things change."

He was right. In this particular case, the competitive salesperson was promoted and moved out of the territory. A new salesperson took over, and he just didn't have the same relationship or personality that the first one did. The customer began looking for other options, and I was there. I began to grow the business when that change happened. Sometimes just being persistent when the potential is worth it will be the most effective strategy.

Often too, the more difficult the account is at first, the greater is the potential later on. You've heard the saying that the bigger they are, the harder they fall. It's been my experience that the obverse of that is true also. Often the harder they fall; the bigger they are once they fall. Let me give you an example of what I mean by that. When I was selling hospital supplies, I visited a medium-sized hospital for the first time. The materials manager saw me. I did my presentation -- who we are, what we did, and why they should care. He looked at me after I was done and he said, "Young man, we don't know much about your company at this point, but what we do know we don't like. Secondly, we have too many suppliers. We don't need another one. We're trying to rid ourselves of some of the suppliers we have. So I'd suggest you go away and not come back."

I thought, "OK. This is going to be a challenge."

I opted for one of the strategies that I discussed here. I visited the account again, about six weeks later. I was able to see the same individual again. This time, I brought in my most powerful product, the product that everybody purchased from us because it was such a great value. It was an item called suction tubing. Suction tubing in a hospital is a staple item that is used throughout the hospital, in almost every department. Hospitals cannot function without it.

We had an arrangement with the largest manufacturer in the world and we had great prices and a good range of different packages and sizes. Our line really was a great value. So, I came back in with my ace product, and presented our suction tubing program. He looked at me and said, "We don't use any." When he said that, we were sitting in his office in the basement and I looked out the open door to his office out into the hallway and there, just outside the door, was a cart. On the cart was suction tubing. I could see it. He knew I could see it. He was lying, I knew he was lying and he knew that I knew that he was lying.

9. Developing Account Strategies

I thought, "Hmmm. This is going to be difficult." What he was doing was protecting the relationship he had with his vendor -- my competitor. This was one of these accounts that was in the hands of a competitor and was not going to give me much conversation because they were protecting that relationship.

I eventually found someone else in the account that I could work with – someone who was a bit more open-minded. I persistently presented my products until an opportunity opened up. The primary vendor, my competitor, had a backorder on a product. We were able to supply it because we were positioned as, "Let us be your backup." We were. We came through, and that led to an opportunity, which led to an opportunity, which led to an opportunity.

Eventually, three years later, that particular hospital was my best account. Now they were protecting me when I was on the inside, just as they were protecting my competitor when I was on the outside. In some cases, when the account is large enough or the potential is great enough, it's worth hanging in there and being persistent.

Terms

strategy – a series of steps designed to bring your prospect or customer from where they are now to where you want them to be

enticer – a small purchase; an easy thing for your customer to buy or to try that opens the door for you in that account.

open-ended question – a question for which there is no right or wrong answer, and one in which the customer must explain *opportunity* – a need or interest your prospect/customer has in your product or service.

TEN

10. Expanding the Business With Customers

Objective

In this chapter, we're going to focus on the other two steps of the main sales processes: turning a customer into a client and client into a partner. We'll discuss those strategies and identify some situations that you are likely to encounter when you first begin your sales territory. Finally, we'll discuss some strategies for dealing with each of those situations.

Remember, a customer is an account that has purchased something. A client is a person or account that has purchased several times. A partner, of course, is that person or account that buys everything they can from you.

I'm going to assume that you have some customers, people who have purchased from your company, that you inherited when you were assigned your sales territory. When you visit those customers for the first time, you're likely to find three different situations. We'll identify each of those situations, and describe appropriate responses from you.

Three common situations

The first situation is characterized by a customer who buys something from you on a regular basis. This account is really a client, not just a customer. You're likely to find some of them.

Another situation you're likely to encounter is a new customer, someone who has purchased for the first time. Maybe this is someone that you converted from a prospect into a customer, or maybe it's someone who had just begun purchasing from your company prior to your involvement as the salesperson assigned to that account. Regardless, the account has purchased once or twice, and they are a new customer. That's situation number two.

The third situation occurs when you discover an inactive customer. An inactive customer is someone who has purchased in the past and for some reason has stopped purchasing. This account is not now buying from your company although it did previously. Often you'll run into these accounts unexpectedly. They are on your customer list. Maybe there are some sales that appear on the computer printout. When you visit them, you discover that several months ago they stopped buying from your company.

How do you deal with each of these? What are your strategies? Let's discuss each one individually.

Dealing with the client account

Let's begin with that client that you inherited, that account that buys something on a regular basis from your company. How do you

10. Expanding the Business With Customers

proceed with them?

Here's a strategy for them. First, spend time to get to know them well. It is easier to learn about them, because they are already of the mindset to be open and honest with you. They already have a relationship with your company. You are coming into the account with some power and credibility behind you.

You do this for two reasons. First, it's easy to do, and in the first few months of your job, you need all the successes you can find.

Second, it's going to provide you ammunition, which you can use in selling to other customers. The more you know about one customer of a specific type -- how they operate, what their concerns are, how they use your product -- the more credibility that knowledge gives you when you call on others of the same type.

For example, let's say that you call on independent lumberyards. You come to know one very, very well. You understand their applications for your products. You discover their problems and the issues with which they are concerned. You learn some of the language they use to describe their customers, their problems, and their processes. Many of those applications, problems and issues are going to be similar to those experienced by other independent lumberyards. If you can spend time getting to know this one at deeper levels, then you can transfer that knowledge to others.

You can appear to the others to be very knowledgeable and credible, and that gives you power in the account. One way you gain power in your territory is by learning about the type of businesses that you're calling on, and then using that knowledge when you speak to others of that same type.

The second strategy for clients is to methodically present everything that you can supply this customer. Don't assume that this customer knows everything you sell. The truth is that most of your customers are not aware of everything that they could be buying from you. Most of them see you and your company through a limited perspective. The glasses through which they view you are focused on only the products and services that you currently sell them. Perhaps you have a hundred different items you can sell them and they're regularly buying two of those items. Chances are they do not know that they can buy most of the other 98 items from you. They don't know that you have them. Believe it or not, most customers only see you as being a competent supplier for what they're currently buying from you.

The easiest and fastest way to grow your business is to take to your clients other items that they could be purchasing from you. You'd be amazed at how often they'll say, "Oh I didn't know you had that. Yes, we're buying that from so and so. What's your deal? We'd just as soon buy it from you." It's a fast and an easy way to grow the business.

To execute this strategy, analyze what they have purchased from you, and then methodically present everything else that they could be buying from you. Each time you see that particular customer,

10. Expanding the Business With Customers

you ought to have one or two other items in your prepared to discuss with them. This is, of all the techniques grow your bus.. rapidly, your single most effective strategy.

To summarize, for someone who buys regularly, a client that you have inherited, you will be most effective implementing two strategies: 1. get to know them as well as possible and you use that knowledge in other places; 2. methodically present item after item, showing them everything they can purchase from you.

New Customers

How about a new customer? What do you do with a new customer? This is an account that may have purchased for the first time from you, or may have just begun purchasing from your company prior to your tenure.

Your overall strategy will be to eventually move them from being a customer or a one-time purchaser to being a client, someone who purchases several items regularly, and then to move them to become a partner with you. As you recall, a partner is an account that buys everything they can from you.

How do you do that? How do you take this one-time purchaser and expand the business with them so that they're buying more and more from you? You follow the pattern for a PROF sales call. PROF is an acronym that stands for Problem-solving, Relationship-building, Opportunity-identifying, Follow-up call. This special sales call follows a specific format.

Once some customer has purchased from you for the first time, call them and make an appointment. At the time you make that appointment, articulate your agenda to them. The agenda is to review their experience with the new purchase, and then to discuss other opportunities. When the customer says yes to the appointment, he or she has given you permission to pursue that particular agenda.

During the call itself, first identify problems and confirm satisfaction with their purchase. Let's say they bought some green widgets from you. Begin the conversation, once you've established some rapport, by exploring their experience with your green widgets. "How did the green widgets go? Are they being used appropriately? Are they working well for you? Was the delivery on time? Was the invoice the way you expected it? Was everything satisfactory with our part of that transaction?"

When you ask these questions, what you're really trying to do is get the customer to express their satisfaction to you. You must get them to say, "Yes. Yes. Yes. Yes." You want to hear a couple of yeses.

What happens if the answer isn't yes? You asked, "How are those green widgets working for you? Are they working out OK?" The customer responded, "No. As a matter of fact we're having problems." What do you do then? Haven't you just blown the whole thing away? No. Not at all. You've just identified a great opportunity. What you do is identify the problem and work to fix it.

You say, "Oh. What is the problem?" Your customer replies,

10. Expanding the Business With Customers

"Well, the people in the production area are getting them mixed in with the blue widgets and they don't understand the difference between them." You say, "Ah. OK. Well, how about if I meet with the production people and give them some pointers as to how to pick out the differences so that won't be a problem in the future." Your customer says, "That's a good idea. Let's arrange for that."

What you have done is this: You have identified a problem and then you have offered a solution. Your customer now sees that you really are concerned, not just with getting the order, but with helping him or her in his business. You are helping your customer use the product that you're selling.

So don't be upset if you hear a "no" when you ask if the customer is satisfied. In fact those no's can be great opportunities to build the relationship and prove yourself to your customer.

There was a study done some time ago wherein the researchers looked at two different situations. In the first situation, a company had purchased a new product from a new vendor and everything went perfectly. The researchers identified a number of those situations and then measured the incidence of that company reordering again in the future from that vendor.

In the second situation studied, the company bought for the first time from a new vendor and there was some problem with the order. It didn't work out quite the way it was supposed to. The sales person came in, inquired, discovered the problem, apologized, and fixed it.

The researchers then measured the incidence of reorder from those customers. They discovered that there was a tremendous difference between the likelihood of the companies representing each of the two situations purchasing more in the future. Interestingly, the people who had a problem where in the salesperson came in, identified the problem, apologized, and fixed it, were far more likely to reorder in the future than those companies who had no problem at all.

Why is that? Doesn't that go against common sense? The answer is no. What happens when you go in, identify a problem, apologize, and fix it, is that the customer then learns what you will do in the worst set of circumstances. You are a known entity at this point. If everything is perfect the first time, they still don't know what you will do if something goes wrong. You are more of a risk than the company that inquires, apologizes and fixes the problem

So, don't be upset if the customer says, "No. It wasn't totally satisfactory." Instead, recognize that as a great opportunity to prove yourself. Remember, you are in it for the long run. Prove yourself and build on that event. Use it as an opportunity to create the perception in the customer's mind that you are a trustworthy, reliable vendor.

So, if there is a problem, you fix it, and then you come back and pick up the conversation where you left it.

You come back a second time and say, "How are those widgets working for you?" This time he says, "Yes. They're working fine." You now have heard the yes that you were hoping for.

10. Expanding the Business With Customers

We are back in our PROF sales call. The first thing on your agenda was to hear the customer confirm satisfaction. Sometimes you have to go off and fix a problem and then come back, and sometimes you hear that confirmation of satisfaction immediately. Regardless, we're back at the point where you're saying to the customer, "Was everything satisfactory?" and the customer is saying, "Yes."

It is important that your customer voice that yes. It is much stronger if it's verbalized than if it is assumed or implied. When your customer says "Yes," he or she is taking a position. You will later build on that position. So, work to hear him or her say, "Yes. I was satisfied."

After having attained that, your next step is to probe the relationship. First, you identified any problems regarding the transaction and solved them. Then you probed the relationship. Ask something like this: "How do you feel about working with our company? How has that gone? Are you satisfied with the way our two companies have worked together?" This is a bigger issue than just the transaction. Ideally, you'll hear your customer say yes again, "Yes. You guys are fine. Customer service took the order fine. Yes, it looks like you are a pretty good supplier. Yes." If your customer says that, confirming his/her satisfaction with the relationship, you are now more powerfully positioned to leverage that satisfaction in order to open other opportunities.

Now, you move onto the second part of your agenda: identifying additional opportunities. You say something like this: "Good. I'm glad you're satisfied. Now, let's discuss other opportunities. What other challenges are you facing that we may be able to help with? What other problems are you having? What other applications can I look at it?"

Since your customer first said yes to you regarding his/her satisfaction, it is now very difficult to say "No" to other opportunities. It would be difficult for your customer to say at this point, "Well I'm very satisfied with everything you've done, but we're not going to give you any other opportunities." That doesn't make sense. If he's satisfied, it just naturally follows that he would want to look with you at other opportunities for other products. That's why it is important that you hear your customer voice the words, "Yes. I'm satisfied."

Encourage your customer to talk about other potential products he can purchase from you. Note them and then make an appointment to come back and discuss one or more of those in detail. Why not do it now? Because you're in it for the long run. Every interaction is an additional opportunity to build the relationship. Try to come back and spend another half hour with him or her to build the relationship, to dig deeper, and to understand the account more completely. Make an appointment to come back at a later time and investigate the opportunity in more detail.

One other way of leveraging some value from this sales call is to ask for referrals. After all, if your customer is happy with your service, happy with your company, happy with the product, happy with the transaction, happy with the relationship, then it just naturally follows that your customer should refer you to other people for whom y[ou] do the same thing. When you think about asking for opportunities, you're really asking for two kinds. Internal opportunities, which are opportunities to sell more stuff to this customer, and external opportunities, which are similar kinds of companies this customer can refer you to.

Let's review this new customer strategy. It revolves around making a PROF call. That stands for Problem-solving, Relationship-building, Opportunity-identifying, Follow-up call. Communicate the agenda to the customer, asking for an appointment. At that meeting, first confirm the customer's satisfaction. If there are problems, fix them and carry on. If there are no problems, encourage him or her to say, "Yes. I'm satisfied." Next, probe the relationship, seeking evidence of satisfaction as well. Then, leverage that voiced satisfaction by asking for other opportunities within this account, other opportunities, outside the account.

Finally, end this sales call with an appointment to pursue those opportunities in more detail.

Inactive Customers

Ok. What do you do with an inactive customer? Again, you're likely to find these as you begin working throughout your territory. You may think they are customers and you discover when you see them that they are inactive. They are no longer buying. What do you do with that situation? Do you go away and say, "Oh. Gee. They decided not to buy from us anymore?" No. Here's what you do.

First, you find out why they stopped buying. You do this in a humble and inquiring way as opposed to a defensive way. You position yourself as someone who is sincerely interested. You can use your newness in your job as a very legitimate reason to be sincerely interested. Let's say that you visit the customer the first time and he says, "No. We haven't bought that from you for six months. We decided to buy it from your competitor." You're stunned, you weren't expecting that. You can say something like, "Oh. Gee. I'm sorry to hear that. You know I'm new in this job and I'm new in this territory and it would really help me to understand what went into that decision. Can you tell me why that happened?"

You appear very humble, and get them talking about why they stopped buying from your company. Sometimes there are lingering issues. "You know the reason we stopped buying from you is because we got that delivery of two by fours that was damaged and no one ever came to pick them up. We still have them sitting in the back lot." You can fix that. Take it back, do whatever needs to be done to remove that burr under their saddle. Get rid of it.

Then you have a clean playing field and you can start fresh. Find out if there are any lingering issues and get them fixed.

Then you treat them like a prospect. You act as if they never have purchased in the past, and proceed accordingly.

Terms

inactive customer – someone who has purchased in the past

10. Expanding the Business With Customers

and for some reason has stopped purchasing.

PROF – Problem-solving, Relationship-building, Opportunity-identifying, Follow-up call.

lingering issue – a problem or question within the customer's organization which has not been resolved to the customer's satisfaction.

6.

ELEVEN

11. Managing Your Territory

Objective

In this chapter, we're going to examine strategies and tactics for managing your territory. In the previous chapters we focused upon the issues related to your interaction with one individual or one account. We examined your face-to-face interactions with customers and prospects and how you should manage those in each individual account. Now we're going to group all of those accounts and people together and examine how to organize the composite, which is your territory.

Your territory is a combination of a number of different accounts, prospects, customers, clients and partners; and all the individuals within them, scattered about in a certain geographical area. Your job is to manage all of those in such a way that you're operating in the most effective way possible. You can be tremendously talented and effective during a single sales call, but if you cannot manage your territory in such a way as to get in front of the highest potential customers in the most efficient manner, you will find it difficult to be successful as a field salesperson.

So, the question is: How do you manage this combination of customers, clients, and prospects in a way that is most efficient and effective?

As I look back on my experience with tens of thousands of salespeople as well as my own personal experience, I've identified three stages of development for the typical new salesperson. It's entirely likely that you will experience these three different stages in your time/territory commitments as you go through your first year or so in your territory.

Three phases

Stage one, which begins with your first few days in the job and extends for several months, is characterized by not having enough to do. You may, for example, have your day planned. You plan to see ten customers, and you feel that should take you the entire day. Unfortunately, you discover that five of them won't see you, and three others don't have any time for you. You only managed to see two of the ten, and you were finished by eleven o'clock. You started out at seven-thirty or eight with the best of intentions, and now it's eleven in the morning, and you are out of things to do.

You just didn't have enough to do. That's very common at first. Beginning in your first few months and extending through your first year or so, you will be in that stage. In this first stage, your challenge is to create a sufficient quantity of people with whom you can work. You have to create a sufficient quantity of relationships so that you will have enough to do and your day isn't spent wondering what you should do next.

11. Managing Your Territory

When you get to that point, you'll progress to stage two. That occurs when you are at capacity. In other words, you're putting in full days, you're seeing your customers and your prospects, you're making good progress and you're working 45-50 hours per week. That's capacity. You're active in your territory, your days are full; you are making progress and things are fairly smooth. You're doing well. That generally will happen somewhere between the tenth month and around the twentieth month, depending on the maturity of your territory and your product lines.

Then comes stage three. Stage three occurs when you are overwhelmed. You have discovered that there is too much to do and you just can't do it all. You have been successful in building up the business, creating relationships, and identifying and pursuing opportunities to the point where you're overwhelmed. You can't get it all done.

Those three stages of activity are predictable and very common in outsides sales. Stage one, not enough to do; state two, capacity; stage three, overwhelmed.

Here's how this works in the real world. Here's an example, again from my days of selling hospital supplies. When I started in my territory, I had a number of prospects and a few customers, all of which were hospitals of various sizes. My Detroit-area territory included the medical center in downtown Detroit as well as some accounts in the northern and eastern suburbs.

One of the largest hospitals in my territory was Harper Grace

Hospital. For the first six months or so of my involvement in that territory it was very difficult for me to see anyone at Harper Grace Hospital. I may have averaged an hour a month in that account. And most of that was invested in unsuccessful attempts to see someone.

My experience at Harper Grace was typical of every one of my accounts. For the first few months, I didn't have enough to do, because I didn't know anyone. I couldn't get people to see me, and those who did wouldn't spend much time with me. I was often finished at eleven o'clock.

Eventually, I became successful in figuring out how to sell to Harper Grace as well as other hospitals. As a result, I began to make more important contacts, develop more opportunities, and, therefore, spend more time in those accounts. At some point, I was comfortably at capacity. I was visiting Harper Grace once a week; spending about an hour each visit.

My calendar was full, I was making a good income and thing were going well. I began to be even more successful. My third and fourth year in that territory, I was spending a half-day twice a week in that account, Tuesday mornings and Thursday afternoons. Why? Because it was a large account and I was successful in penetrating it. The relationships and opportunities in that account created more and more demands for my time and my involvement.

The process was repeated within most of my accounts. At that point, in my fourth and fifth year, I was overwhelmed. The fifth year I was so overwhelmed that I began to hire part-time help to help me administratively because I had too much to do and not enough time to do it.

That's an example of why you go through these three stages. You start out with people not wanting to see you, not thinking very highly of you, and not knowing you very well, but as you create relationships and dig in to your accounts, you discover that your territory, and therefore, your work, expands. At some point, you become overwhelmed.

Strategies for Each Phase:

At each of the three stages of progression in your territory, you need a different strategy to deal with the primary problem at that stage.

You begin at stage one. You probably don't have enough to do. You probably are not incredibly busy all day long. What's your strategy? Two fold – first, work to establish some systems and disciplines now that will help you when you get to the next two levels. Second, create, as quickly as possible, a base of people who you can work with -- a group of customers who like to see you, will be honest with you, will show you opportunities and listen to you

Developing systems and disciplines

There are several management systems that, if you can discipline yourself to implement them now, will help you create positive habits, which will serve you extremely well later on.

The first of these is the discipline of planning for your territory coverage. Start by planning your sales calls four to five weeks ahead.

This planning can be fairly general: I'll be in Detroit the first week, Cleveland the second, etc.

Then, each week, tightly plan for four out of the next five days. Repeat this every week. Keep the fifth day open for those things that pop up; those opportunities that you can't work in any other time. Use that as your buffer to fill in.

Next, develop loops within your territory. In other words, don't drive from Point A to Point C and then backwards and then forwards. Instead, try to arrange your sales calls so that you start from your home base, making your first and last call of the day nearest your starting point. Your mid-day calls should be the furthest away so that your route forms a loop, with the furthest customer at the end of the loop. Generally, plan to be at that customer before or after lunchtime. Then work your way back, making calls all along the way back. Each day is a loop, or if you're traveling a large territory spending nights out, then each two or three days is a loop.

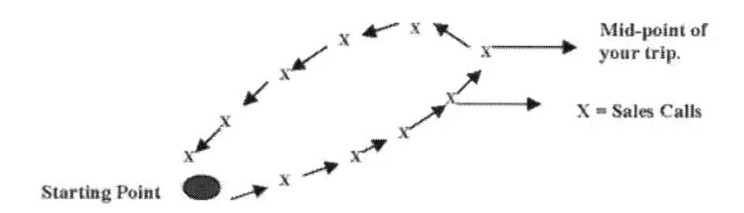

Don't schedule yourself too tightly. Make "–ish" appointments. In other words, don't say, "I will see you at ten," say, "I'll see you at ten-ish on Tuesday." The reason you do that is because so much of your time is not totally in your control. You may have an eight o'clock appointment and you think, "I'll be done by nine. Twenty minutes to get there, so I'll make the next appointment for nine-thirty." Do you know how many times you're not out of there by nine? Or you're out of there at eight-forty instead of nine? Your best-laid plans don't always work. So you give yourself some flexibility throughout the course of the day by making appointments that are not specific at ten, but ten-ish. That way, if you're done early, you can come in at a quarter of and still be on time and you can come in at a quarter after and still be on time. This relieves a lot of stress and anxiety from your life.

Activity goals

In the first few months, when you're searching around for people to work with, you'll find it helpful to establish activity goals for yourself.

A sales goal is a goal for which there are measurable results. You determine to sell a certain number of dollars of this product, or so much to that account. These results are often measured by your company's computer, and you normally have access to the reports. It's difficult, in the first stage of your territory management, to create accurate sales goals because you have few relationships, little knowledge of the territory, and virtually no history on which to base them.

An activity goal, on the other hand, focuses on the quantity of the key activities that must occur if you are to make sales. Think about the different things that you must do in order to make a sale. Certainly you must make a first call on a new prospect. That first call on a new prospect is an activity. You must complete a certain number of those in order to turn some of them into qualified prospects, and you must turn a sufficient number of them into qualified prospects in order to turn some of them into customers.

While, at this point, you cannot predict how much you are going to sell, you can give yourself a goal for how many first calls on new prospects you want to make, understanding that you must make a certain number of them to be successful in your job. A first call on a new prospect is one type of key activity.

Another key activity might be the presentation of a product to a prospect. If you are going to sell anything, you must present that thing. And you must present it a number of times to a number of prospects to give yourself a change of selling more than one. A presentation, then, is another key activity. Still another might be a slight variation of this -- the presentation of a product to a customer.

So, we have identified three different kinds of key activities: first calls on new prospects, presentations to new prospects, presentations to customers. Those are just examples. Your actual list of key activities could go on and on.

In the first few months of your work in your territory, you should give yourself goals for the quantity of each of those key activities you would like to complete. In other words, you say, "This week I'm going to make first calls on twenty prospects, and I'm going to make product presentations to five of those prospects, and I'm going to make product presentations to ten customers." Those are three different activities, each having a quantitative goal.

11. Managing Your Territory

Once you have created those activity goals, you then plan to complete that quantity of activities. This is a good way to direct your energies in the early months because it will drive you to focus on the right kinds of activities. And out of those activities will eventually arise the people with whom you will do business.

To some degree, no matter what you sell or at what point you are in the development of your skills, there is always a part of sales success that is driven by numbers – by the quantity of activity. Given everything else being equal, the sales person who makes ten product presentations a day is going to sell more than the one who makes eight. Make sure that you are driving yourself to the right quantity of key activities.

The illustration below is a typical chart used to create activity goals, and then to keep track of your progress on those goals.

Other disciplines: Paperwork

Attend to the paperwork in a disciplined and rigorous way from day one. Pay particular attention to those account profiles, personal profiles and contact logs because they form the information base on which you will proceed for the next few years. As you get busier and busier, your tendency will be to let paperwork go to the last moment, or to do it sloppily. That will get you in trouble because you will begin to forget things and opportunities will drop through the cracks. Right now, while you have the time, create the discipline to always attend to the paperwork in a thorough, disciplined, and methodical way.

Build the discipline of not always immediately reacting. What I mean by that is particularly now, when you have more time, you will have a natural tendency to immediately react to the stated or implied problems of your customers. Let's say you stop in the office for fifteen minutes to pick something up after which you have five sales calls planned. When you get into the office there's a note there, "Call such and such customer. They've got a problem." You call them and your customer says, "We're having a problem with this product."

Your natural tendency is to immediately react. So, you drop everything, put off your sales calls and try to fix that problem. At one

Example

	Creating A Customer (Calls on Suspects or Prospects)				Expanding the Business (Calls on Customers)		
	First Visit	Opportunity Identified	Proposal	Close	Additional Opportunity Identified	Proposal	Close
Weekly Goal	10	6	4	2	2	2	1
Actual	ꟷꟷꟷ ꟷꟷꟷ ꟷꟷꟷ	ꟷꟷꟷ ꟷ	ꟷꟷꟷꟷ	ꟷꟷ	ꟷ	ꟷ	ꟷ

level, that's perfectly appropriate, because it is part of the service that you provide -- to attend to the problems of your customers. But, on another level, it interferes with you effectively managing your territory because it takes that portion of the day that you had planned and destroys it.

What do you do? Instead of always immediately reacting, you ask your customer this question, "I'm going to have time to deal with this problem on Tuesday, will that be OK?" In effect, you say to the

11. Managing Your Territory

customer, "Can I work on this problem at a time that is more convenient for me other than right now?" You'll discover if you ask that question, seeking permission to handle it later, you'll discover that about 50 percent of the time what you thought was a crisis really was not. Half the time the customer will say something like this: "Yes, you can take care of it next week." When your customer gives you that permission, then you have gained back control of your day and control of your territory.

Sometimes your customer will say something like this: "No, this is urgent. I've got a problem; I need to get it fixed." If that is the case, then fix it. That's the price you pay. The battle for managing your time is a daily battle. You're not going to win every battle.

However, when you always assume that the problem is urgent and always immediately react, you always give up control of your day to whoever happens to be on the other end of the phone.

Finally, the last discipline is to be careful about what you do for your customers, and be careful about what you do for your associates inside your business. Take the long-range perspective. At some point in time you're going to have too much to do and not enough time to do it. At that time, it will be great if the people around you, your customers and your associates, do what they can to take as much off of you as possible. Train them now.

For example, when I started in my career as a distributor salesperson, I told my customers that I wasn't there to take orders. I would not pick up an order. I wouldn't write one down. I'd say, "Call that in. My job is not to be a clerk and write down orders. There are people in my office who can take the order over the phone better than I can. I want you to call them and tell them. I'm here to help you solve your problems, to help you reach your objectives. I don't want to waste my time in a clerical function writing down orders."

Some people thought that was horrible, but I trained my customers to call the orders in and not bother me with the details of that clerical function. You can do something like that. I'm not saying you should refuse to take orders. I'm saying you should think about what you train your customers to expect of you and take the long-range perspective right now. Train them to not see you as a clerk.

The same thing is true for your associates inside your business. If you get everybody in your business in the habit of expecting you to do half of their work for them, to complete those credit applications, to write up those purchase orders, whatever it is, if you train them to expect you to do it, then a year and half from now, when you have too much to do, they will still expect you to do those things. Instead, train your customers and train your associates right now while you have time. Take it off of you and delegate it subtlety to them because at some point in time, you're going to have too much to do. You're going to be overwhelmed with the business that you create.

Terms

territory – a combination of a number of different accounts, prospects, customers, clients and partners; and all the individuals within them scattered about in a certain geographical area

11. Managing Your Territory

loops – planned trips throughout your territory that begin and end at the same place, and have the most distant contact at mid-point in the trip.

sales goal – a goal for which there are measurable results

activity goal – focuses on the quantity of the key activities that must occur if you are to make sales.

TWELVE

12. Managing Yourself

Objective

In this final chapter, we're going to change the focus. In the earlier chapters, we discussed strategies and tactics for interacting with your customers and your prospects. The focus was on how to interact with those in the outside world.

In this chapter we're going to turn inward, and discuss the challenge of managing yourself. Our objective is to provide you with tools to master this difficult challenge.

In my first full-time field sales position, as I was spending hours in the car driving, I came to the conclusion that about half of the challenge of my job as an outside salesperson had to do with my customers and my prospects. The other half, fully 50 percent of my success, had to do with the way I dealt with myself; the way I managed my thoughts, my feelings, and my energy.

That part of my success had to do with the way I made the best use of my greatest asset – me! I have since come to believe even more fervently that the primary factor in the success, or lack thereof, of an outside salesperson, is that person's ability to manage himself or

12. Managing Yourself

More of everything.

The rapidly expanding body of information contains the threat of you becoming overwhelmed and rendered ineffective by the sheer weight of the information that you must manage.

In order for you to be effective, you will need to create systems to stay organized. You will need to stay on top of the organization of the information about your accounts, your products, your projects, your prices, etc.

If you don't, it will take only a very short time for you to discover yourself wasting time, being inefficient because you haven't been organized. Through several different chapters, we have discussed the need to take good notes, to be prepared, and to spend time with your account profiles. That's because it is such an important issue.

The need for continual organization is a thread that runs from beginning to end, through the entire sales process, and wraps your job together. Let it unravel and you become unraveled. Keep it tightly wound, tightly organized, and you'll find yourself to be far more effective. Stay organized. That's number one.

Deal with absolute integrity

Deal with everyone with absolute integrity. Why is that? Wouldn't you rather deal with someone you trust than someone you don't? I'm sure that's the case. I'm sure that there have been times when you refused to do business with someone even though they might have had the best product and the best price. You didn't do business with them because you didn't trust them. People want to do business with people they trust. If you're going to be successful, you must manage yourself by a certain code of ethics that reveals your integrity.

Here's an example. My next-door neighbor had been having his lawn done by a fertilization company for years, and his front yard always looked much better than mine. I eventually got to the point where I was embarrassed about it. So I got the name of the company that did his lawn. I called the company, having already decided to purchase their services. I wanted my lawn to look as good as my neighbor's.

I called the company and said, "What I would like to do is have you come out and do your thing and then maybe leave me a brochure or something, indicating what my options are. I'm sure you have several different packages." The salesman said, "Yes, we'll do that.." I said, "Ok, when will you be out?" "We'll be out next week, and then we'll leave you a brochure with all your options in it." I said, "Great, that's just what I want." Then he said, "And you can cancel anytime you want."

I said, "Wait a minute. I'm not subscribing today. I'm making no commitment; I just want you to come out one time and then leave me a brochure so I can decide what to do." He said, "Well, yeah, OK. We'll do that and you can cancel anytime because once we come out that means you have subscribed but you can cancel anytime." I said, "Wait, wait, wait, wait. No, no. That's not what I...no, don't. No."

12. Managing Yourself

What was happening was this: I was beginning to mistrust the salesperson. He first said, "Yes, we'll do just what you want. That's OK." Then he slid in this idea that what I'm really doing is committing for the season. No, I'm not. It wasn't the product and it wasn't the service and it wasn't the price and it wasn't the company. I just didn't trust the salesperson. I wound up saying, "No," and hung up. Here I was, as ready to buy as I could possibly be, and yet I didn't. The reason? I felt uneasy with the salesperson.

That kind of thing happens frequently. It happens with your customers, too. You can have the greatest product, the greatest service, and the greatest company, but if your customers don't trust you, then they are not going to buy from you.

This issue of dealing with absolute integrity is two things. It is, first, good business, because when you deal with integrity you develop in your customers a sense of trust in you. That's good business. Integrity is also, I believe, a moral absolute. I think part of how you live your life is to live it with absolute integrity. That's part of managing yourself.

Ten Commandments for the Ethical Salesperson

Here are my Ten Commandments for the Ethical Salesperson. Ten rules that will guide you as you manage yourself to operate with absolute integrity.

The First Commandment – Don't intentionally misrepresent anything, ever, to anyone. Period. That's clear enough.

The Second Commandment – Fix any important misunderstandings that you can. Occasionally you'll run into situations where a customer will have a misunderstanding. That misunderstanding may work to your benefit. For example, the customer thinks that your competitor's product doesn't do something and you know that it does. They've misunderstood. In order to be ethical, whenever you're aware of an important misunderstanding, you need to correct that misunderstanding. You need to let the customer know what the truth is, even if it reflects poorly on your offering, or takes away some advantage that you have.

The Third Commandment – Work hard for your employer. There are times when you can sleep in and make your first call at ten instead of eight. There are times when you can be done at three instead of five. There are times when you can take a two-hour lunch break. However, your employer has made a commitment to you to provide you an opportunity, to provide you an income, to provide you a place to work, a company to associate with, and you have an obligation to your employer to work as hard as you can for your employer. Don't give in to the temptation to cut corners. Instead, obey Commandment Three for the Ethical Salesman, and work hard for your employer.

The Fourth Commandment – Always be willing to trade a short-term loss for the sake of a long-term gain. There are times when you can get a sale, or make some progress in the short-term by compromising on the long-term. You can, for example, take a piece of business on the basis of a misunderstanding. You can take advantage

12. Managing Yourself

of some untruth, some misunderstanding. That's a short-term gain that in the long-term will hurt your reputation. I'd rather you walk away from that business, that short-term gain, for the sake of building a reputation that will last long-term. That's Commandment Four.

The Fifth Commandment – Do what you say you're going to do. That sounds so simple, but it is not nearly as easy it sounds. Remember, you are in it for the long-term, you are building trust, and you are building a reputation as an individual. Part of that reputation is a perception on the part of your customers that they can depend on you. You must, therefore, be dependable. That means that you must do what you say you're going to do. If you make a promise, you better be organized enough to remember it, to follow through on it, and to be diligent enough to make it happen.

On the other hand, you must never over promise. Don't say you'll have it here next week when you know that's impossible. Then you can't do what you say you're going to do. Under promise, don't over promise, and be organized enough to follow through everything you say you're going to do. That's the next commandment.

The Sixth Commandment – Give liberally. I believe that as an outside salesperson you are in a special situation. You're in a situation where you have more freedom, more challenge, more opportunity for fulfillment, more opportunity for a lifetime of personal development, and more opportunity for higher income than most of the population. Most people would love to have your freedom, your opportunity, your income, your challenge, and your interesting, challenging always-different job.

That means that you are one of the blessed people in our society. And because you have been given more, you have an ethical obligation to give more. That doesn't mean just money. I think you have an obligation to give of your time, as well as your money, to those people and groups and organizations that can benefit from it. My friend Nido Qubein says that, "Service is the rent you pay for the position you occupy." You occupy a higher position than most, and therefore, own more rent. Whether it's Boy Scouts or the local church, you are probably associated with organizations that can use some of what you have. If you're going to be an ethical salesperson, you need to give liberally.

The Seventh Commandment – Recognize those who help you. There is a natural tendency on the part of outside salespeople to think that you're a maverick, that you've done it all by yourself. After all, you spend most of the day by yourself. You are the one making those sales calls. Under these circumstances, it's easy to think that you alone are totally responsible for whatever success you have. The truth is that you have a manager who helps, directs, and guides you. You have support associates back in your office, who, because they do their job, enable you to do yours. Your company is full of people who have contributed to your success. For you to think that you've done it yourself is untrue and unethical. Recognize those who help you.

The Eighth Commandment – continuously learn and improve. There is a natural tendency for you to plateau at some point in time, a

12. Managing Yourself

couple years from now, and think you've learned it all, and have all the answers. When that happens, it often signifies the death of personal growth. Your ability to change, grow and improve is one of the most significant core success skills that you'll have during the rest of your career. When you stop learning and stop improving, you start sliding downhill. That's unethical.

When your company hired you, they hired not only the skills that you brought with you, but also the potential that you have. They expected that you would grow to become more competent and skilled than the day you were hired. When you think you have learned it all, when you plateau, you rob your employer of the potential for which they hired you. That's unethical.

I believe that you owe yourself and your employer continuous effort to improve, to be more effective and more competent. That's ethical.

The Ninth Commandment – never give up. This does not mean that you should never make a sound business decision to stop spending time at an account in which you are making no progress. That's just business. Rather, I'm talking about giving up on your abilities, giving up on your opportunities, and giving up on your ambition to create positive things. It usually means giving in to negative thoughts, and allowing yourself to be depressed and discouraged. I think when you give up, you're being unethical. Never give up.

The Tenth Commandment – don't speak badly about anyone.

That includes even your most devious, incompetent competitors. Don't ever speak badly about them. If you come across a customer who is complaining about how poorly a competitor behaves, don't even agree with them. Your customers understand that if you speak badly about a competitor, you'll speak badly about your customers. And nobody likes to be around people who talk about them behind their backs. So, don't ever speak badly about anyone. It's unethical.

Learn optimism

In the 1990s, Dr. Martin Seligman authored a book entitled Learned Optimism. I believe it is a landmark book. In it, Dr. Seligman talks about his life work as a research psychologist. He began working with dogs. The researchers placed dogs in a cage from which they could not escape, and then subjected them to mild shocks. The dogs would try to get out, and discover that they could not do so. Eventually they learned that they could not get out of the cage and would give up and lay down.

The researchers would then arrange the cage in such a way that one of the sides was down. Again, they would place the dog in the cage, and subject it to mild shocks. The dogs would not walk out, but instead would just give up and lay down.

Dr. Seligman postulated that the dogs had learned hopelessness. Once they had this attitude of hopelessness, they would not even recognize the obvious way out of their dilemma.

Dr. Seligman eventually began to experiment with human

beings. He put them in a room and subjected them to irritating noises. There were knobs and switches in the room, and the people would experiment with them in an attempt to turn the noise off. They soon discovered that they could not do so. At that point, like the dogs, they would give up and just sit there and accept their dilemma.

Later, the researcher would again place those people in the same room. However, this time one of the switches was wired to turn off the noise. The people would not even try. They had learned helplessness and hopelessness.

Eventually, Dr. Seligman theorized that people learn optimism and pessimism. He discovered that there is a significant difference in the success people achieve in life as a result of their optimism or lack of it. Those people who learn to look on life optimistically become far more successful than those people who learn to look at life pessimistically. Seligman refined this concept to the point where he could analyze speeches by politician, assess their optimism quotient, and thereby predict the winner of elections. The more optimistic of the two politicians invariably won the elections. He discovered that he could apply this even to athletic contests. He would analyze the interviews of the players beforehand, and those who had the most optimistic outlook were predictably on the winning teams. So, he came to the conclusion that one's life is far more fulfilling and successful as a result of an optimistic outlook than a pessimistic perspective.

The book contains a survey that readers can use to test themselves in regards to the degree of optimism and pessimism in their minds.

You can apply this concept to yourself and your sales position. Suppose you have a bad call, where everything goes wrong. Your customer announces that he is taking all your business away from you and giving it to your competitor, is severing relationships and never wants to see you again. As you walk out of that account you realize that 10 to 15 percent of your income is gone. That's a bad call.

You can choose to deal with this difficult event in two ways. You can choose to view this optimistically or pessimistically. Let's say you look at it pessimistically. You say to yourself, "I really blew it. I mishandled this account. I mishandle all my accounts. I'll never understand how to do this job right." Having thought that to yourself, how much energy and enthusiasm do you take to your next sales call? None, if you're even able to make the next sales call. You have yourself so depressed by your thoughts that you have no energy.

Now, let's suppose that you made exactly the same sales call and exactly the same thing happened. As you walk out to your car, you say to yourself, "They made a mistake. Good thing it's just this one account. Good thing it's only temporary; they'll realize their mistake and in a few months they'll come back to me and start doing business with us again. Good thing it's just them and it's just temporary." If you say that to yourself, now how much energy and enthusiasm do you have for your next sales call? A whole lot more than if you thought all those pessimistic things.

Here's the point behind all of this. It wasn't the event that was

12. Managing Yourself

the problem; it was the way you thought about the event. You explained it to yourself in a pessimistic way or you explained to yourself in an optimistic way. If your explanation was pessimist, you have no energy, no enthusiasm, and no drive. You're not going to be successful the rest of the day. If you continue in this mindset, you are not going to ever be successful. However, if you explain it optimistically, you have all of your enthusiasm, energy and drive, and that will enable and empower you to be more successful.

You can see, then, that much of your success depends on how you think about what happens to you. So it is in life and so it is in sales. As an outside salesperson, you're going to have lots of miserable days. You're going to have lots of depressing days. You're going to have lots of rejection; you are going to hear lots of no's; you're going to have lots of adversity and lots of failure. It comes with the territory. The issue, however, is not so much that it happens, but rather how you choose to think about it when it happens.

And, you can choose your thoughts. What an empowering truth! You can choose to think pessimistically or you can choose to think optimistically. You can choose your thoughts.

If you're going to manage yourself effectively, if you're going to do well with this person with whom you'll be spending most of your time, you need to manage your thoughts to choose optimism instead of pessimism. If you choose optimism, you will be more successful than if you choose pessimism. If you choose pessimism, you won't. It's that simple. Learn optimism.

12. Managing Yourself

those customer service people has a friendly relationship with you and will be a friendly, comforting voice. That can change your day -- just having a phone conversation with a friendly, likable person who cares about you.

Of course, think about your family and your friends as people who can support you in this effort to manage yourself.

Fifty percent of your time and much of the battle of being a successful outside salesperson depends not necessarily on your ability to manage and interact with the world, but also on your ability to manage yourself.

As you go forward from here, concentrate just as much on dealing with yourself as you do on dealing with the world.

Terms

integrity – the quality of being true to who you are: In sales, it means operating with absolute honesty and reliability.

ethics – rules of behavior which define right and wrong for a salesperson.

learned optimism – a book title by Dr. Martin Seligman, as well as the name for characteristic of

thinking in a certain way about adverse experiences so that you increase your success.

support system – a group of people surrounding a salesperson who can be counted on to support and encourage him/her.

ABOUT THE AUTHOR...

Dave is a consultant and speaker who helps his clients grow their sales and develop their people. Specializing in business-to-business selling situations, Dave creates effective sales systems and helps salespeople take their performance up a level.

He's acquired his message through real-life experience. Dave has been the number one salesperson in the country for two different companies in two distinct industries.

As the general manager of a start-up company, Dave directed that company's growth from $10,000 in monthly sales to over $200,000 in just 38 months.

Dave annually presents over 75 seminars and training programs. He has spoken in 47 states and 11 countries, and has authored 13 books.

He holds a B.A. degree from the University of Toledo, and a Master's from Bowling Green State University.

He and his wife live in Grand Rapids, MI and Sarasota, FL where he is a father, a step-father, an adoptive father, a foster father, and a grandfather.

Dave is a member of the Author's Guild, the Christian Businessmen's Committee, and the American Society For Training and Development.

He can be reached at:

Dave Kahle Management, LLC

Grand Rapids, MI and Sarasota FL

PO Box 523, Comstock Park, MI 39432

(800) 331-1287

(616) 451-9377

info@davekahle.com

www.DaveKahle.com

12. Managing Yourself

Dave Kahle is available to:
- Speak at your conference or convention.
- Create customized sales training programs for your outside sales force, inside sales force, or sales managers.
- Consult with you on issues relating to sales productivity.

Dave Kahle is available to speak with your group or help your business grow. Visit The Biblical Business Course: www.thesalesresourcecenter.com

and take a class to begin your growth. Visit: www.biblicalbusinessresourcecenter.com

Dave Kahle Management, LLC
Grand Rapids, MI and Sarasota FL
PO Box 523, Comstock Park, MI 39432
(616) 451.9377 www.davekahle.com

Made in the USA
Lexington, KY
17 March 2018